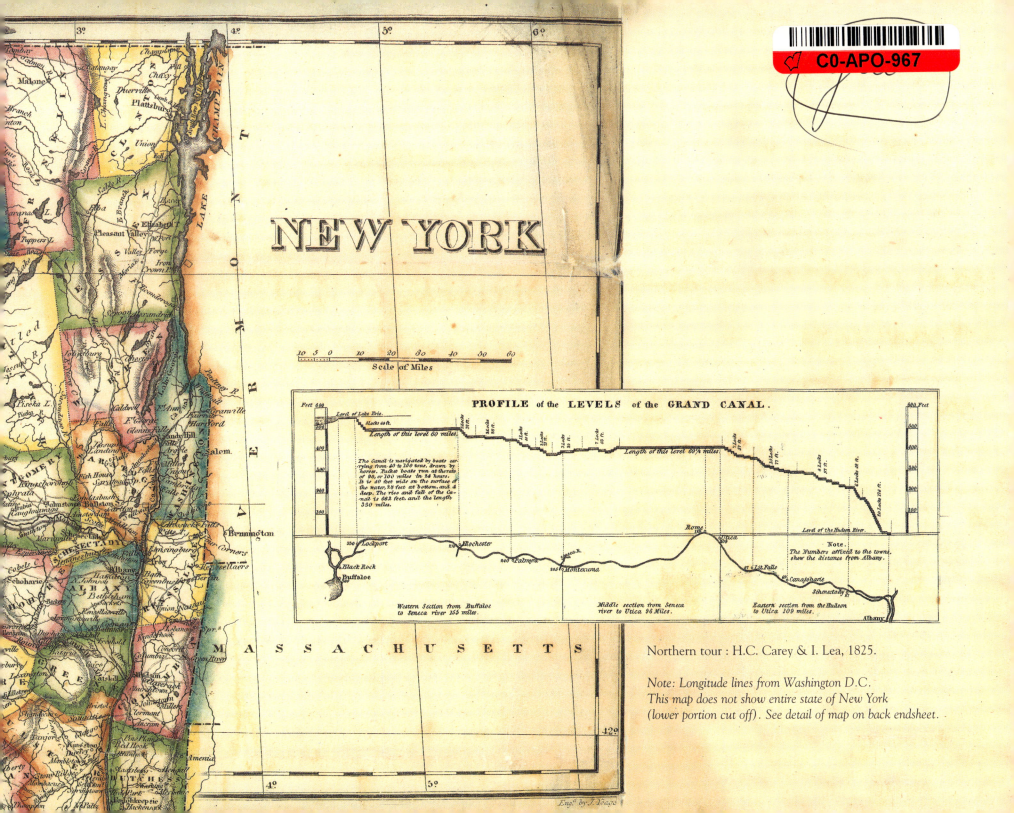

Northern tour : H.C. Carey & I. Lea, 1825.

Note: Longitude lines from Washington D.C.
This map does not show entire state of New York
(lower portion cut off). See detail of map on back endsheet.

Near Cumorah's Hill

IMAGES OF THE RESTORATION

Near Cumorah's Hill

IMAGES OF THE RESTORATION

PHOTOGRAPHS & TEXT BY
PAUL E. GILBERT & DOUGLAS L. POWELL

Covenant Communications, Inc.

Editorial note: Minor corrections in spelling and punctuation have been made to clarify quoted material.

Published by Covenant Communications, Inc., American Fork, Utah
Book and jacket design by Jessica A. Warner
Copyright © 2000 Photographs and text by Paul E. Gilbert and Douglas L. Powell
All rights reserved. No part of this book may be reproduced in any form or by any means without permission in writing from the publisher.

Printed in Hong Kong
First Printing: October 2000

07 06 05 04 03 02 01 00   10 9 8 7 6 5 4 3 2 1

ISBN 1-57734-743-9

Library of Congress Cataloging-in-Publication Data

Gilbert, Paul, 1955-
    Near Cumorah's Hill / Paul Gilbert, Douglas Powell.
        p.   cm.
    Includes bibliographical references.
    ISBN 1-57734-743-9
    1. Mormon Church—New York (State)—Cumorah, Hill, Region—History—19th Century.. 2. Cumorah, Hill, Region (N.Y.)—Pictorial works.
    I. Powell, Douglas, 1963-   II. Title.
    BX8615.N5 G55 2000
    289.3'747'0222--dc21   00-058980
                                        CIP

Contents

ACKNOWLEDGMENTS vi

PHOTOGRAPHER'S NOTE vii

AUTHOR'S NOTE viii

INTRODUCTION ix

CHAPTER ONE
A Land of Promise 1

CHAPTER TWO
Palmyra 11

CHAPTER THREE
Suddenly a Light Descended 27

CHAPTER FOUR
Cumorah's Hill 39

CHAPTER FIVE
Sacred Places 51

CHAPTER SIX
Susquehanna and the Great Bend 65

CHAPTER SEVEN
The Whole Church of Christ in a Little Old Log
House 83

CHAPTER EIGHT
Colesville and South Bainbridge 97

CHAPTER NINE
Spiritual Manifestations in Mendon 107

ENDNOTES 116

PHOTO CREDITS 120

Acknowledgements

This work represents over ten years of effort by many people. We wish to acknowledge and thank:

- Elder Philip Clark, former Director of Church Sites, and Elder Jerry Hess, current Director of Church sites, for their help in accessing these sites and for their keen interest in the images.

- J. Sheldon Fisher, former director of the Rochester Historical Society Museum, whose enthusiasm for the Mormon story never fades.

- Irene Havens, whose family owned the Brigham Young home site after the Youngs left the property over 150 years ago.

- David and Kathleen Cook of Pittsford, New York, whose insight and stories further enhanced our project.

- Sandy Robbins of The Pro Lab in Denver, Colorado for helping produce many of these images. Also, Spiro Nichols of Nichols Photo Lab in Salt Lake City, Michael Snelson of Snelsons Photo Color in Springville, Utah, J. Ryne Hazen of the Color Pro Lab in North Salt Lake, and Borge Andersen of Borge Andersen & Associates in Salt Lake City.

- Ronald Rubin of Rubin & Zimmerman, P.C. of Denver, Colorado who were especially helpful as we prepared to publish this work.

- Jordan & Tracy Powell for their help with research.

- Mack and Jackie Sumner for reviewing the manuscript, and for their advice and encouragement.

- The Scott Air Force Base library staff for their assistance in helping procure many of the books that were used for reference.

- Charles Decker, the Afton town historian for his assistance with sites in the Colesville area.

- Preston Pierce, Ontario County Historian, and Ed Varno, Director of Ontario County Historical Society, for their assistance in obtaining information on the Canandaigua region.

A very special thanks to my parents for encouraging my early interests in photography and accepting my interest and faith in the LDS Church. My deepest love and appreciation for my wife, June, who constantly encouraged and promoted my work. Without her companionship and motivation I simply couldn't have done this. And to my children for their love and support.

P.G.

A very special thanks to my family, particularly my parents, my eternal sweetheart, and my children.

D.P.

Photographer's Note

I went to New York to complete a degree in photography at Rochester Institute of Technology. Like many people, I thought New York would be a concrete jungle . . . skyscrapers, noisy traffic, yellow cabs, etc. However, I soon came to adopt the slogan, "I love New York," because to me it came to mean green, lush valleys, hills, mountains, waterfalls, lakes, rivers, canyons, gorges, gorgeous fall colors, and a rich history of many significant events that affect us profoundly today.

One of the first things I did upon arriving in New York State was to visit Palmyra, the Hill Cumorah, the Smith Farm, and the Sacred Grove. I love the calm, peaceful feeling that exists in these places, and I love the reverent feelings they evoke for sacred events that took place over 150 years ago. How humbling it is to be in these places where so much happened.

When family and friends came to visit, we took them to see the "Church Sites." But there were many family members and friends who, for one reason or another, were unable to visit. Because these sites became so dear to me, I wanted to share them. But I didn't want to just document the sites; I wanted images that conveyed my feelings when I visited the Sacred Grove or the Hill Cumorah. What a challenge! The trees in the Sacred Grove are tall and close together, which makes it one of the most difficult places to photograph. I have literally spent over one hundred hours there in the hopes of creating visuals that are both satisfactory and beautiful.

In the late 1980s, I was doing some photography work for the Mendon Historical Society. The historian learned that I was a member of the LDS Church and gave me a copy of Sheldon Fisher's account of his archeological dig at the Brigham Young home site. I came to realize that there were lots of little-known stories, and I needed the help of someone who could research and write these stories.

Around this time, Doug Powell came to Rochester to work on his medical residency in dermatology at Strong Hospital. He was very much into the outdoors and we became fast friends, and would often go photographing together. Doug has a gift for giving great talks, and a knack for telling a good story. He became interested in the project and eventually agreed to do the writing. He discovered many fascinating stories that begged for visualization, and he became the driving force that motivated us to complete the project.

We wanted this book to be both a historical and visual experience, one that you will enjoy displaying in your home, or using as a reference on trips to historical Church sites. We also hope its contents will increase your understanding and testimony of the events that occurred in upstate New York, near Cumorah's Hill.

Paul Gilbert

▼ *Schuler Falls. One of many waterfalls found in the Finger Lake region of upstate New York. These deep gorges and tall waterfalls created by streams that run northward into Lake Ontario present a stunning contrast to the rolling hills of this region.*

Author's Note

▲ *The azure blue waters of Seneca Lake became a baptismal font for many early converts.*

When Paul told me about his plans for a photo book of LDS Church historical sites in New York state and asked me to write the text, I was excited and very interested. As I began to read extensively about Church history in the New York region, I fell in love with the history and stories of those associated with the Restoration.

If there is anyone in this book with whom I can relate, it is Josiah Stowell. While searching for a lost Spanish silver mine, Josiah came in contact with Joseph Smith, a prophet of God. The treasure he found and cherished for the rest of his life was far more precious than silver—it was a testimony that Joseph was a prophet of God, and that the Book of Mormon was the word of God. Imagine my joy when I discovered that Josiah was a distant cousin of one of my great-grandfathers.

My own search for "treasures" while working on this project has been rewarded with moving insights and strengthened convictions regarding the Restoration that began not far from the Hill Cumorah.

I remember sitting along the side of the road between the towns of Colesville and Harmony and thinking about Joseph and Oliver fleeing to escape the fury of the Colesville mobs. Joseph and Oliver had done nothing to deserve this treatment—except to preach the restored Gospel. It reminded me that the Savior Himself was likewise persecuted for teaching the truth.

While studying about Joseph's trips to the Hill Cumorah, I could almost sense his feelings as he removed the rounded lid from the stone box, and saw the gold plates for the first time. Later, while reading about the night, four years later, when he went to retrieve those plates, my heart went out to Emma. During my research, I saw a painting by Robert Barrett that depicts Emma holding the team of horses near the base of the hill in the middle of the night. She waited by herself while Joseph went to get the plates, and I realized then that her days of waiting for Joseph were just beginning. What a great and "elect" lady.

I am grateful to the men and women who sacrificed their farms, their families, their time, their reputations, and even their lives to follow a prophet of God and bring the blessings of the restored gospel to us. My words cannot adequately describe my gratitude for Joseph Smith. Perhaps the hymn "Praise to the Man" by W.W. Phelps says it best. Most of all, I am grateful to our Father in Heaven and his Son, Jesus Christ, who appeared to the young Joseph in a grove of trees, and who still direct us and communicate with us through a living prophet.

My hope is that those who see the images and read the pages in this book will be moved to learn more about the events and people involved in the restoration of the Lord's kingdom near Cumorah's Hill.

Douglas Powell

Introduction

Personal revelation has always been available to God's children individually, but for the people as a whole, God chooses prophets to transmit His will and direction. Nevertheless, there have been times when this communication was lost because people turned their backs on God. During these times, the spiritual light of revelation turned into the darkness of despair.[1]

In the meridian of times, Jesus Christ, the Only Begotten Son of the Father, descended from His heavenly throne to live on earth, thus dispelling one of these dark times.[2] Jesus Christ brought His gospel of love to replace the Law of Moses, organized a church with apostles and prophets, and, in an incomprehensible manner, suffered and died in order to save all mankind from physical and spiritual death if they would but obey His law.[3]

After His resurrection and ascension into heaven, His chosen apostles continued to receive revelation and guide the people, but they foresaw times when members of the Church would again turn their ears from the truth, precipitating a "falling away" (2 Thessalonians 2:3).[4]

These early apostles also foresaw a day when lost blessings would once again be restored to the earth,[5] when heavenly and earthly things would be gathered together in the "dispensation of the fulness of times" (Ephesians 1:10). Hundreds of years prior to the spring of 1820, the spiritual darkness that covered the earth had already begun to dissipate. "But always, as it had from the beginning, the Spirit of God inspired worthy souls."[6] Courageous men, noting discrepancies between what they understood from reading the Bible, and what they were taught by established religion, started to contend for their convictions, sometimes at the risk of their livelihoods and lives. On 31 October 1517, Martin Luther posted his 95 *Theses* on the door of Castle Church in Wittenberg, Germany, and the movement known as "the Reformation" began.[7] Joseph Fielding Smith, tenth president of The Church of Jesus Christ of Latter-day Saints, noted:

> In preparation for [the] restoration the Lord raised up noble men, such as Luther, Calvin, Knox, and others whom we call reformers, and gave them power to [break] the shackles which bound the people and denied them the sacred right to worship God according to the dictates of conscience. . . .
>
> Latter-day Saints pay all honor to these great and fearless reformers, who shattered the fetters which bound the religious world. The Lord was their Protector in this mission, which was fraught with many perils. In that day, however, the time had not come for the restoration of the fulness of the gospel. The work of the reformers was of great importance, but it was a preparatory work.[8]

The desire of these reformers to make the scriptures available to the common man, coupled with

▲ *"One of them spake unto me, calling me by name, and said—pointing to the other— 'This is my Beloved Son, hear Him.'"*[9]

▶ *(Opposite page) Niagara Falls. "We halted a short time to view this wonder of nature, and to adore that God who had formed a world so sublimely grand. The leaping of a mighty river of waters over a perpendicular fall . . . the foaming and dashing of its white spray upon the rocks beneath . . . all conspired to fill the contemplative mind with wonder and admiration, and with reverence to the Great Author of all the wonders of creation."[10]*

the development of the book-printing process by the mid-fifteenth century in Europe, made the words of Christ and the prophets available to anyone who sought them. No longer did people need to rely on traditions and clergy to learn of the Lord's ways.[11]

Likewise, a land was prepared for the "fulness of times." The ancient prophet Nephi, in the Book of Mormon, was taught by the Lord that the land which we now know as the Americas is a land of promise, "a land which is choice above all other lands" (1 Nephi 2:20). The Lord promised Nephi's father, Lehi, that he and his seed would obtain this land of promise if they were righteous. Lehi left Jerusalem with his family, traversed the desert wilderness, crossed the sea by boat, and settled at last in the land that, according to at least one scholar, geographically matches Central America.[12] With them, they carried a record of ancient scripture to teach them of the Lord's ways.

Eventually their descendants were visited by the resurrected Savior Himself who taught them His gospel. Nephi saw in vision, however, a time when his people would fall away from the gospel of Christ, and the land would be given to another people.

> And I looked and beheld a man [Columbus] among the Gentiles, who was separated from the seed of my brethren by the many waters; and I beheld the Spirit of God, that it came down and wrought upon the man; and he went forth upon the many waters, even unto the seed of my brethren, who were in the promised land.
>
> And it came to pass that I beheld the Spirit of God, that it wrought upon other Gentiles; and they went forth out of captivity, upon the many waters.
>
> And it came to pass that I beheld many multitudes of the Gentiles upon the land of promise (1 Nephi 13:12-14).[13]

As a result of the Reformation and in direct fulfillment of Nephi's prophecy, seekers of religious freedom from many nations came to this land of promise.

The Reformation, while remarkable, significant, and enlightening, paled in comparison with the light that broke forth on "the morning of a beautiful, clear day early in the spring of eighteen hundred and twenty."[14] On that day, an unassuming fourteen-year-old boy who simply desired to know which church was correct was visited by God the Father and His Son Jesus Christ, and was chosen to be God's prophet in the latter days. Revelation resumed, priesthood authority was restored, commandments were given, ordinances were revealed, and temples were built. In addition, another testament of Jesus Christ, the Book of Mormon, came forth and preceded the organization of a church led by apostles and prophets. This was the restoration of God's kingdom, the stone spoken of by Daniel of old, "cut out of the mountain without hands," which stone would fill the earth. "And in the days of these kings shall the God of heaven set up a kingdom, which shall never be destroyed: and the kingdom shall not be left to other people, but it shall break in pieces and consume all these kingdoms, and it shall stand for ever" (Daniel 2:44-45).

No place on earth was better prepared for the events of the restoration of the gospel than the small Finger Lakes region of western New York, around Palmyra, in the early 1800s. In a country where freedom of religion was protected by the Constitution, the state of New York had even adopted its own articles of religious tolerance.[15] Religion was on the minds of the people, and great manifestations of their beliefs were visible in their lives. As noted by one Carl Carmer, "In no other area of the western hemisphere have so many evidences of an existence transcending mortal living been manifest."[16]

Near Cumorah's Hill, in western New York, the message and the "blessings of old"[17] would begin in a grove of trees and spread until they filled the earth. President Gordon B. Hinckley has said:

> God spoke to His prophet in parting the curtains on this the dispensation of the Fulness of Times. He introduced His Beloved Son, our Savior, our Redeemer . . . and told him to listen to Him. That marked the beginning of this work. That beginning is different from the beginning of any other church on the earth. It is unique and different and we never need be ashamed of it. We have to be very, very grateful for it and acknowledge it and live up to its teachings.[18]

It is not necessary to visit the Sacred Grove to know that Joseph truly did see God the Father and His Son there. It is not necessary to stand on top of the Hill Cumorah to obtain a witness of the truthfulness of the Book of Mormon. Nor is it essential to know the approximate location of the appearance of Peter, James, and John to Joseph and Oliver to realize that the priesthood of God has been restored to earth. The simple process given by James in his epistle, which Joseph Smith put to the test in the grove of trees, is enough: "If any of you lack wisdom, let him ask of God, that giveth to all men liberally . . . and it shall be given him" (James 1:5).

"... when the sun first rose upon this new land, a spirit of the earth saw it and thought it so beautiful that he laid his hands upon the ground to bless it. The hollows left by his fingers filled with water and became the Finger Lakes."

INDIAN LEGEND

Sunset over the Finger Lakes reveals the long, thin reflections (from near to far) of Skaneateles, Owasco, Cayuga, and Seneca Lakes.

CHAPTER ONE
A Land of Promise

(Opposite page) At 215 feet, Taughannock Falls, located near the southern tip of Cayuga Lake, is the highest waterfall east of the Rocky Mountains. Its autumn-thin veil of water is shown here in resplendent fall colors.

The Genesee River has carved its path through Letchworth State Park, NY (known as the "Grand Canyon of the East"), creating three stunning waterfalls. Shown below is Letchworth Upper Falls.

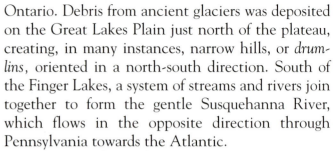

One of the most striking topographic features of western New York is a cluster of long, thin, parallel lakes known as the Finger Lakes. Created anciently by the northward retreat of glaciers, these bodies of water are carved out of an ancient, eroded plateau known as the Appalachian Upland.[1] Indian folklore states that "when the sun first rose upon this new land, a spirit of the earth saw it and thought it so beautiful that he laid his hands upon the ground to bless it. The hollows left by his fingers filled with water and became the Finger Lakes."[2]

The rolling hills of this region are frequently interrupted with deep gorges and tall waterfalls created by streams that run northward into Lake Ontario. Debris from ancient glaciers was deposited on the Great Lakes Plain just north of the plateau, creating, in many instances, narrow hills, or *drumlins,* oriented in a north-south direction. South of the Finger Lakes, a system of streams and rivers join together to form the gentle Susquehanna River, which flows in the opposite direction through Pennsylvania towards the Atlantic.

Today, much of the Finger Lakes region is a patchwork of farms and pastures because the soil is rich and well suited for growing; however, in earlier times the hills were heavily forested and nearly inaccessible to the settlers. Frontier settlements were also vulnerable to attack from the French-supported Iroquois Indians.[3]

After the Revolutionary War, the Indians who remained in western New York signed a peace treaty with the continental United States in 1783.[4] By this time, their influence on the developing nation was minimal; still, their impact on the early settlers in the New York region was significant, as they taught the newcomers how to hunt, trap, clear forests, and live in the wilderness.[5]

Before the Revolutionary War, the early British colonies often received charters allowing them to extend their respective boundaries to the Pacific Ocean, as was the case with both Massachusetts and Connecticut. The charters given to Massachusetts and Connecticut also granted both of them rights to the land west of the colonies, although the Dutch were already settled there, and *they* claimed the land.[6] The rights of sovereignty over western New York were left in dispute; however, a compromise was eventually achieved, with each state receiving an area of land.[7]

Wanting to avoid further difficulties from this compromise, Massachusetts promptly sold its tract of six million acres. Two wealthy speculators, Oliver Phelps and Nathanial Gorham, bought the vast tract of land in western New York for less than three cents an acre.[8] The law still required them to also purchase the land from the original owners, the Indians, so Phelps quickly headed west to run surveys and obtain the title of the land from the remaining Iroquois. In July 1788, a council fire was held at Buffalo Creek, and 2.5 million acres were sold to the investors for $5000.[9] Phelps then promptly laid out townships of six square miles and opened one of the first land offices in the United States at Canandaigua Lake, the head of one of the Finger Lakes.

Unfortunately, all did not go well for Phelps and Gorham; many of their backers failed them, and they were required to give two-thirds of the land back to Massachusetts. Robert Morris, a financier of the Revolution, purchased one million acres from Phelps and Gorham, but he too ran into financial difficulty and went bankrupt.[10]

Nevertheless, the floodgates had opened for settlers looking for new land and a new start.

In 1789 the first permanent immigrants of the region arrived, settling in two locations: in an area west of Canandaigua Lake, and in the town of Farmington, just a few miles west of the Joseph Smith farm.[11] Initially, migration was slow, but by 1795 the movement had become one of the greatest land rushes of its time.[12]

The Dutch and the Germans had been the earliest settlers in eastern New York's Hudson River Valley, but the great majority of those who moved to western New York were from New England, where the population

HEART OF THE REGION

If there was any place in western New York that could have been described as "the heart of the region" during the land rush around 1800, it would have been Canandaigua. From the time that it became one of the first land offices in the United States, and the seat for the county that covered much of western New York, the town thrived with the immigration of settlers. Located at the top of beautiful Canandaigua Lake, the wonders of the village were lauded. Horatio Spafford claimed that "in point of beauty and elegance of position, as well as in the style of its buildings, Canandaigua is excelled by no place of the same extent in the United States."[1]

1. Horatio Gates Spafford, *A Gazetteer of the State of New York* (Albany, New York: B.D. Packard, 1824; reprint Interlaken, New York: Heart of the Lake Publishing, 1981), 302.

was quickly outgrowing the available land. By the turn of the century, an average of more than one hundred sleighs per week reputedly passed through the town of Geneva, headed for the Genesee Country, the name given to the land between Seneca Lake and the Genesee River.[13] Genesee Country was the most famed location in the new frontier because of its rich soil and widespread promotion among the settlers. Elkanah Watson described the emigrants going to this land as "swarming into these fertile regions in shoals, like the ancient Israelites, seeking the land of promise."[14]

The first main artery of travel to this country, the "Genesee Road" followed the Mohawk River to the town of Utica, after which it passed along the north ends of the Finger Lakes, ultimately becoming the route of today's N.Y. Route 5.[15] Lucy Mack Smith's description of traveling through Utica indicates that this was the road traveled by the Smith family as they migrated to western New York. Later, other roads and turnpikes facilitated travel, and the construction of the great water highway known as the Erie Canal made travel even easier.

In 1788 a frontiersman called "Indian Allen" and his brother-in-law built a grist mill near the great falls on the Genesee River. The following year, Allen became the first resident of what would become

 (Opposite page) Early on, the rolling hills of the "Genesee Country" became the most famous sector of the New York frontier due to the lavish stories of fertile land. This field of flowers is on a small hill that lies just north of the Sacred Grove.

(Opposite page) The sun sets over the "Genesee Country" as seen from the top of the Hill Cumorah where, in the 1800s, emigrants were "swarming into these fertile regions in shoals, like the ancient Israelites, seeking the land of promise."[16]

▼ *A rock commemorating one of the treaties between the Americans and the Iroquois Indians is situated in front of the historic Canandaigua Courthouse. These treaties allowed speculators such as Oliver Phelps and Nathanial Gorham to purchase land—thus opening the doors for settlers.*

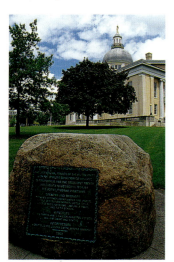

LAKEVILLE MORMON BARN

In 1797, Roger and Sarah Wattles moved to the Genesee country and built a cabin between the villages of Lakeville and Geneseo. Their son, David, stayed on the homestead and in 1827 was appointed Postmaster of Lakeville by John Quincy Adams.

Because the Wattles' home was on the crossroads of two major stagecoach routes, the barn behind their house became a place of gathering and shelter for travelers needing a place to rest. According to tradition, David's wife, Sarah, who had lived in Vermont before their marriage, was somehow related to Joseph Smith, and had heard about him. Thus, in the 1830s when traveling missionaries spoke of Joseph Smith, Sarah took the time to listen. Meetings were held in the barn, where the missionaries taught the local people about the restored gospel. It is even reputed that Joseph Smith came here to preach, and "people from all sections, especially from Lakeville, attended these meetings to hear Joseph speak."[1] Samuel Smith, Joseph Sr., and

Lucy were also named as having visited the old barn.

Although these reports cannot be verified, Joseph and Samuel did travel throughout this region while teaching the gospel, and Joseph Sr. and Lucy accompanied Samuel on some of his journeys. This gathering place would have been a likely place for them to teach. Undoubtedly, the restored gospel was taught there, which is how it received the name "Mormon Barn."

Today the barn still stands about a mile west of Lakeville, on Highway 20A. The house that stands in front of it is the original homestead of the Wattles, which also served as the first post office of the region. The barn is steadily deteriorating, but the message that was taught there over 170 years ago continues to flourish and spread throughout the world.

1. Lois Dickerson Wilkins. *The Mormon Barn at Lakeville, New York* (self-published: Lakeville, New York, 1978), 24.

FROM FLOUR TO FLOWERS

When the Erie Canal was constructed across New York, few cities benefitted more from it than Rochester. Accessible transportation, power generated by the cascading falls, and fertile wheat-growing soil in the surrounding country attracted millers in large numbers; by the 1830s Rochester was known as the "Flour City." In 1816 (when the Smiths moved to Palmyra), Rochester, with a population of 331, was possibly smaller than Palmyra, but by the time the gold plates were translated, Rochester had grown to over 11,000 people. When E. B. Grandin initially refused to publish the Book of Mormon, Joseph Smith went to the publishers in the larger city of Rochester in search of help. However, when Joseph eventually succeeded in persuading Grandin to publish the book in Palmyra, the "Flour City" was bypassed as the home for the publication of the Book of Mormon: more than 100 million copies would be published over the next 170 years.

In time, Rochester's flour mills disappeared, but the excellent growing environment made the city a favored place for nurseries, transforming the "Flour City" to the "Flower City," which continues to blossom and thrive.[1] Rochester is also known for several historic figures, such as Jenny Jerome, Winston Churchill's mother, who was born here; Frederick Douglass, who expounded his views here; and Susan B. Anthony, who sought for women's rights here.

1. Blake McKelvey, *A Panoramic History of Rochester and Monroe County, New York* (Woodland Hills: Windsor Publications, 1979), 51-68.

Rochester. The mill did poorly and was abandoned, but others who came later, particularly Colonel Nathaniel Rochester (a former Maryland businessman and legislator), could see the advantage created by the falls. In 1803, in conjunction with two other speculators, Nathaniel Rochester purchased the land around the falls on the Genesee River and laid out a city with sites for mills, a future courthouse, and lots so affordable that settlers would be attracted to the area. His plan succeeded, and the city of Rochester was born.[17]

For Rochester and western New York, the Erie canal "served as a lifeline in the fullest sense as it pumped new blood into the frontier and gave it strength."[18] Some of the "new blood" which came through Rochester in the early 1800s would not only give life to the frontier, but would help give life to the restored Church.

By the year 1810, six years before the Joseph Smith Sr. family arrived in Palmyra, 50,000 people lived in the Genesee Country, and by 1820, the year of the First Vision, 100,000 people lived there.[19]

PARLEY P. PRATT

With the loss of the family farm in Oswego, New York, twenty-year-old Parley P. Pratt headed west in 1826, pausing in Rochester long enough to buy a small pocket Bible. Then he bid "farewell to the civilized world,"[1] and moved on until he arrived at a small settlement about thirty miles west of Cleveland. There, in the dense forest, he built a small hut to protect him from the winter, and while "the wind shook the forest, the wolf howled in the distance, and the owl chimed in harshly to complete the doleful music which seemed to soothe [him]. . . . in [his] little cabin the fire blazed pleasantly, and the Holy Scriptures and a few other books occupied [his] hours of solitude."[2]

In 1827 Parley returned to his childhood home in Caanan, New York, to call upon a young lady he remembered fondly. He soon married Thankful Halsey and the two returned to the small cabin in the forest near Cleveland. Two years later, Parley felt impressed to "forsake [his] house and home for the gospel's sake."[3] Settling all his affairs, he and his wife started on the trip east, but upon arriving in Rochester, Parley was moved to "leave the boat . . . [and] stop awhile in this region. Why, [he] did not know; but so it was plainly manifest by the Spirit to [him] . . . for [he] had a work to do in this region."[4]

When he learned of the Book of Mormon, he was soon baptized, becoming one of the greatest missionaries of the restored Church and one of the Twelve Apostles.

1. *Autobiography of Parley P. Pratt*, ed. Parley P. Pratt (Jr.), (Salt Lake City: Deseret Book, 1979), 9.

2. Ibid., 10.

3. Ibid., 17.

4. Ibid., 18.

◄ *(Opposite page) Richardson Canal House was once a rest stop along the Erie Canal where weary travelers could stop and get refreshments. It is now a favorite restaurant and bed and breakfast.*

CHAPTER TWO

Palmyra

". . . a stranger came along, picked me up, and carried me to the Town of Palmyra." Whoever the stranger was, he carried a boy who was to become a prophet into a town that would become the birthplace of the Restoration.

Palmyra was the closest village to the Smith frame house in Manchester township.

 Detail of the reconstructed barn on the Smith farm. Besides clearing 60 acres for farming, Father Smith and his sons built fences, animal shelters, a barn, a cooper's shop, and possibly a granary and a smokehouse.

12

The year 1816, when Joseph Smith Sr. moved his family from Vermont to New York, was an unusual one. In her history, Lucy Mack Smith describes an "untimely frost . . . that well nigh produced a famine."[1] The foul weather encouraged many Vermonters to follow the same path as the Smiths on their way to New York,[2] but this poor weather was not confined to their small region in Vermont. The cold weather of that year was noted over North America and Europe, and has been attributed to one of the largest volcanic eruptions in recorded history: the eruption of Mount Tambora in the Dutch East Indies in 1815.[3] With frost and snow throughout the summer months over much of the northeast United States, it was a year without a summer.[4]

Given the destruction of the crops by frost, and the reports of the inexpensive, fertile fields of the Genesee country, Joseph Sr. decided to move his family to Palmyra, New York. He arranged for transportation of his family, then went on ahead to make living arrangements. Lucy's overwhelming task was to finish financial arrangements and to take their eight children (the youngest only a few months old) a distance of three hundred miles, some of it snow-covered, by sleigh and wagon to their new home.

Lucy's indomitable spirit is typified by her actions when their less-than-trustworthy driver, Caleb Howard, tried to unload their belongings and take the wagon from them when they were twenty miles west of Utica. In the midst of a large company of travelers, she proclaimed:

> Gentlemen and ladies, please give me your attention for a moment. Now, as there is a God in heaven,

that wagon and horses, as well as the goods that accompany them, are mine. This man is determined to take away from me every means of proceeding on my journey, leaving me with eight little children, utterly destitute. But I forbid you, Mr. Howard, from driving one step with my wagon or horses. And here I declare that the teams, goods, and children, with myself, shall go together to my husband and their father. . . . I shall take charge of my own affairs.[5]

Still lame from the surgery on his leg two years earlier, young Joseph had walked much of the journey to Palmyra in great pain. Seeking respite during the last few miles, the ten-year-old boy found a place to ride in the last sleigh of the caravan with

 Nathan Harris, father of Martin Harris, was another early settler on the north side of Palmyra village. After leaving Rhode Island with his wife in 1793, Nathan purchased 600 acres from John Swift for the price of $300, and located his log home on the north side of Wintergreen Hill (shown above).[6]

which the Smith family traveled. A fellow traveler discovered Joseph resting, roughly pulled him out, and threw him on to the ground. Years later, Joseph described this event: "I was knocked down . . . and left to wallow in my blood until a stranger came along, picked me up, and carried me to the Town of Palmyra."[8] Whoever the stranger was, he carried a boy who was to become a prophet into a town that would become the birthplace of the Restoration.

The Smith family arrived in Palmyra with barely "two cents in money," but their destitute state was quickly forgotten as the family "surrounded their father, clinging to his neck, covering his face with tears and kisses that were heartily reciprocated by him."[9] For Lucy, "the care and affection of a tender husband and father doubly paid me for all I had suffered."[10]

By 1816, the village of Palmyra was no longer a frontier town, but a well-established community.

▲ Nathan Harris eventually turned part of his land over to his son, Martin, a man who willingly sacrificed it to publish the Book of Mormon. Martin initially mortgaged his land in 1829, then had to sell 151 acres in 1831 in order to pay $3,000 to Grandin.[7]

▶ This lake-stone house, built in the 1850s, was constructed on the foundation of Martin Harris's home. Today, it houses missionaries who volunteer their time at Church historic sites.

◀ *Detail of the lake-stone house constructed on the foundation of Martin Harris's home. Martin Harris's home was a one-and-a-half story, white frame house. It burned down in 1849.*

The first lake-stone buildings appeared about 1820, and the last one at about 1858. Those in this area were built by English artisans who came here to work on the locks at the Erie Canal. The stones were laid up as a veneer with a field-stone inner wall. The veneer stones are lake stones selected for size by passing them through a steel ring. Many of the stones for this house were hauled from Lake Ontario, a job which often took several days because of the weight of the load. The stones were meticulously placed in the mortar, with the smoothest stones used for the front of the homes, and the rougher stones used in the back.

Masons never passed their skills on to the next generation, and would stop work if someone came to watch them. The art of masonry could only be learned and passed on through membership in a masonry guild.

15

▶ Until the time of his death in 1823, Alvin Smith was the driving force in the construction of this frame house which he desired as a "pleasant room for father and mother."[11] After Alvin's death, a neighbor, Russell Stoddard, was hired to help finish the construction.

In 1828 Martin Harris paused to sit on the fence surrounding this house as he contemplated in despair his loss of the 116 pages of manuscript. "On coming to the gate, he stopped, instead of passing through, and got upon the fence, and sat there some time with his hat drawn over his eyes."[12]

The original settler of the region, John Swift, purchased the land in 1789 and erected a trading post known as Swift's Landing along Mud Creek. The name of the village was changed to Palmyra in 1797.[13]

Swift died in battle during the War of 1812.[14] By then, the village of Palmyra was no longer a simple trading post but a sizable community with several offices, saddle and harness shops, tailor shops, a blacksmith shop, a tannery, a distillery, shelters for animals, and a schoolhouse.[15]

Because Joseph Sr. had always worked the land in order to provide for his family, it is no surprise that Lucy Smith's history indicates that their intention upon arrival in New York was to "apply all our energies together and endeavor to obtain a piece of land."[16] Lucy's ability to paint oilcloth coverings for tables produced a successful business, which allowed her to replace some of the furniture she had sacrificed by moving to New York.[17] Joseph Sr. opened a "cake and beer shop," where the family sold ginger-

◀ The Smith farm in the winter. On this 100-acre farm, the family planted wheat, corn, beans, and flax. They also planted a large apple orchard of 200 trees.[18]

 Shown here are hewn timbers similar to those that would have been found on the Smith farm. Splitting logs for rails and buildings was familiar work to the Smith boys. Being "Obliged to labor hard for the support of a large family . . . required the exertions of all that were able to render any assistance . . ."[19]

 (Opposite page) This well, located about 100 yards from their frame house, may have been the one that was dug and used by the Smith family.

bread, pies, boiled eggs, root beer, and other popular items.[20] On special occasions, these items were sold on the streets in a mobile handcart. Joseph Sr. and the two oldest boys also hired out for available labor with harvesting, gardening, and well digging.

The family did well enough to "secure a scanty but honest living,"[21] and after approximately two years they were financially able to contract for a hundred-acre farm of their own at a cost of $100 yearly, with the last payment to be due in December of 1825. Now, for the first time since 1803, when they had sold their farm in Tunbridge, Vermont in order to liquidate some debts, Joseph Sr. and Lucy had some land they felt they could call their own. This "nearly wild or unimproved piece of land, mostly covered with standing timber,"[22] lay two miles south of the village of Palmyra, just across the Farmington township line from Palmyra township, and along a rutted wagon path known as Stafford Road.

As part of an ancient forest, this land contained many trees that "grew to tremendous size"; some trees in the forest reached a girth of seven feet or more in diameter and soared to heights of greater than one hundred feet.[23] Waterfowl and small game could be found along the small stream that ran through the land, while trout and spawning salmon swam in the cold, clear waters.[24]

In her history, Lucy stated that in the first year after obtaining the farm, they built a log cabin and cleared land until "something like thirty acres of land were got ready for cultivation."[25] William Smith spoke of "trees which could not be conveniently cut down,"[26] while Joseph Jr. remembered that "it required the exertions of all that were able

Upstairs bedroom in the frame house. The Smiths were not safe from mobs even in the confines of their own home. Once while mother Smith was home alone with her youngest daughter, a mob entered their house. "As [we] were going upstairs, I looked out of the window, and one glance almost turned my head giddy. As far as I could see by the light of two candles and a pair of carriage lamps, the heads of men appeared in every direction, some on foot, some on horseback, and the rest in waggons. I saw that there was no way but for me to sit quietly down, and see my house pillaged . . . However, there was one resource, and to that I applied. I went aside and kneeled down before the Lord."[27] Her son William arrived home just in time to disperse the mob—a direct answer to Lucy's prayer.

(Opposite page) The kitchen in the frame house is where Joseph learned that Martin Harris had lost the initial 116 translated pages. After entering the house and being offered some food, Martin dropped his utensils and in anguish cried, "Oh, I have lost my soul! I have lost my soul!" To this, Joseph replied, "Martin, have you lost that manuscript?"[28]

 The main intersection in the village of Palmyra is unique, being the only city with four different churches on the corners of one intersection.

The churches are Baptist, Methodist, Presbyterian, and Zion Episcopal.

to render any assistance."[29] Clearing thirty acres of forest in one year was a phenomenal accomplishment. The typical method of clearing the land consisted of felling the trees, drying them, burning them, and collecting ashes, which could then be used as fertilizer or made into soap. A skilled woodsman could clear one acre in seven to ten days, but the typical pioneer cleared and sowed only about ten acres the first year.[30] With such arduous work, along with the building of a cabin, it is understandable why young Joseph and the other children "were deprived of the benefit of an education."[31]

Initially, the cabin had only two rooms on ground level and two rooms in the loft, but it pos-

sessed a few luxuries, such as glass windows, wooden floors and doors, a stone fireplace, and a bark-shingle roof.[32] Here, in this seventeen-by-twenty-eight-foot home, ten people (Joseph Sr. and Lucy, Alvin, Hyrum, Sophronia, Joseph Jr., Samuel, William, Catherine, and Don Carlos) ate, slept, and lived, an arrangement that Lucy Mack Smith described as "living comfortably."[33] Later, a sawn-slab bedroom wing was added to accommodate the crowded family.[34] Because it was difficult to determine the exact boundaries of townships in those early days, this cabin was unknowingly constructed on the opposite side of the township line from the Smith farm, fifty feet *inside* the Palmyra township.[35]

A study of the history of this region during this time period is often confusing because the system of townships is unfamiliar to many. A "town," or "township," is a large division of a county, which may actually include one or more villages or cities. The *village* of Palmyra, for example, is included in the larger *town*, or *township*, of Palmyra. The Smith family lived in "Palmyra," that is to say, they lived in the smaller village of Palmyra. However, after their "removal to Manchester,"[36] the family did not live in the actual village of Manchester; they resided in the rural "township" of Manchester, which included other villages as well.

The township of Farmington, where the Smiths farmed, was originally settled in 1789 and saw most of its growth before the year 1820. In 1821, while the Smiths were residing on their farm, the township of Farmington was divided. The west section maintained the name of Farmington, while the east tract, initially named Burt, was renamed Manchester after the principal village.[37]

THE ERIE CANAL

The Erie Canal was the brainchild of Jesse Hawley, a flour merchant living in Geneva. Due to his partner's poor business dealings, he found himself bankrupt in 1806 and fled New York. Taking up residence in Pittsburgh to escape the debts that suddenly settled on his shoulders, he contemplated the state's shipping problems and wrote an essay that was printed in the *Pittsburgh Commonwealth* in December of that same year. Although wheat was grown abundantly in the Genesee Valley, it was both risky and expensive to transport it to the eastern cities. In his essay, Hawley proposed the construction of a canal that would connect Lake Erie, the Mohawk, and the Hudson Rivers. Being a man of integrity, Hawley soon returned to New York and gave himself up to the authorities in Canandaigua because a friend of his had risked bail for him in a lawsuit over Hawley's obligations. Sentenced to debtors' prison, Hawley continued to contemplate a canal that would join the West to the East. He sent a series of fourteen essays to the *Genesee Messenger* newspaper and signed them simply "Hercules," as it was the custom of the day to use pseudonyms when writing to the public.

New York Governor DeWitt Clinton eventually recognized the genius of these essays and the political and monetary value of such a project. In 1816, the same year that the Smiths arrived in Palmyra, the state of New York approved the construction of the Erie Canal. The actual digging of the canal began in 1817 and the project was completed in October 1825, when Governor Clinton dedicated it with great pomp and circumstance. Jesse Hawley was there and Clinton gave him much of the credit for devising the plan for the canal.

To mark this auspicious occasion, a primitive form of the telegraph was devised using a series of cannons positioned within hearing range all along the route of the canal and the Hudson River, from Buffalo to New York City. It took one hour and twenty minutes for all the cannons along the 363-mile route to fire, delivering the message to the waiting crowds eager to celebrate.

We might wonder if the Smiths heard the sounds of the cannons from their rooftop as they were constructing their frame house at around that same time, or if they realized that the canal would bring people to their door to hear the restored gospel.

(Opposite page) A rock wall built around their farm by the Smith boys can still be seen in some spots such as this area on the west side of the Sacred Grove. Part of the wall can also be seen extending up to the parking lot of the Palmyra Temple.

Within the Farmington township, seven to eight miles south of the Smith farm, a prominent industrial village named Manchester arose along the Canandaigua Lake outlet and became the driving force of township growth. By 1820, over 4,000 residents lived in the township. However, the construction of the Erie Canal to the north drove businesses out of Farmington that could not compete with those along the highway of water.[38] Due to its location along the proposed canal route, Palmyra became a boomtown, growing from a population of 1,137 in 1800 to 5,416 in 1830.

Probably no time seemed happier to the family, for they finally had a place where they could stay and prosper—or so they hoped. Instead, the land they had purchased would provide an abundance of spiritual experiences as well as trials. Like Sinai of old, the soil would be sanctified by the presence of those who would visit; but misdeeds and persecutions would eventually drive them from their "hallowed ground." Subsequent chapters detail the joys and sorrows the Smiths experienced during their years in the Palmyra region.

With the departure of the Smith family in 1830, the village of Palmyra remained "free" of Mormons for the next eighty-four years, although some of the negative feelings toward Church members lingered. In June of 1907, George Albert Smith arranged to purchase the Smith farm in Manchester. A family was then sought who could move onto the farm and serve as a liaison for the Church. This family would have to be resilient enough to tolerate persecution, and sociable enough to soften and win the hearts of the people in the region. Church leaders chose Willard Washington Bean and his wife, Rebecca Rosetta Peterson Bean.

Born in May of 1868, Willard Bean grew up with a love of the outdoors, a passion for athleticism, a gift for public speaking, and a fervor for the gospel of Jesus Christ. He picked up the sport of boxing, at which he excelled and became one of the best middle-weight boxers of his time. But unlike most who participated in the sport, he brought a higher standard of living and behavior. Of him it was said, "In each of his diverse professions [boxing and preaching] Bean excels. He talks eloquently and puts more persons to sleep by his punching than by his preaching."[39] He was called "The Fighting Parson."

In September of 1914, Willard married Rebecca, and a few months later they were called by then President of the Church Joseph F. Smith to settle on the Smith Farm, which they did by February, 1915. According to Elder Bean, "I was instructed by the First Presidency that I was going to the most prejudiced spot in the United States if not in the world and to be in no hurry to begin missionary work, but to wait until I made some friends that would be loyal and true."[40]

While living on the Smith farm, the Beans worked the land just as the Smith family had done. They grew crops; maintained herds of horses and cattle; and cared for hundreds of chickens, geese, ducks and guinea hens.[41] Occasionally townspeople rode past the farm to yell at them and tell them to "go back to Utah where they came from."[42] Merchants refused to sell goods to them, requiring the family to drive their buggy to other villages to purchase groceries. At school, their children's desks were initially set apart from the others, and their possessions were sometimes stolen or hidden by other children.

In an attempt to break the ice with their neighbors, Willard offered to put on a boxing exhibition in the town opera house. A ring was built and public announcement was made that he was willing to take on all comers who would step into the ring with him on a given date. On the night of the exhibition, the first few rows of the hall were filled with large men waiting for their chance to fight Willard. The first opponent was knocked out before laying a glove on Brother Bean, and the next six were likewise promptly dispatched. Watching this show, the eighth man (and the rest) decided not to enter the ring.[43]

In spite of the difficulties they faced, the Bean family remained enthusiastic and took every opportunity to become involved in the community and to make friends. What had originally started as a mission call for "five years or more years"[44] became a twenty-four-year period of service for the Beans. During the time of their stay in New York, Brother Bean was instrumental in helping the LDS Church obtain the Martin Harris Farm, the Peter Whitmer farm, and the Hill Cumorah. Perhaps the greatest accomplishment was simply the creation of an amicable environment that would bless the hundreds of missionaries who would serve there. Brother Bean described how the "prejudice . . . melt[ed] away . . . ," as the family gained the respect and love of the community.[45] "The battle for survival has now been won," he said. "Persecution has all but faded out. Nothing more than a faint echo survives."[46]

"This marvelous theophany was unequaled since the events on the Mount of Transfiguration two millennia ago."

PRESIDENT GORDON B. HINCKLEY

A shaft of light shines through the trees in The Sacred Grove, where Joseph Smith received the First Vision.

CHAPTER THREE

Suddenly a Light Descended . . .

The spring of 1819 found the Smith family working to steadily improve their land. They tapped maple trees to produce sugar, and eventually collected one thousand pounds per year.[1] At some point, they planted a large apple orchard on their land. Making a living was difficult during those first few years because the cash crops such as wheat were not yet a reality; income came mostly from making potash or producing cordwood as they cleared the forest. To supplement this, the older boys, including Joseph, did odd jobs in the region and likely resided temporarily where they were working.[2]

After the Smith family's move to the farm, Palmyra was still the village closest to them, and frequent visits were likely. Orsamus Turner, a contemporary of the Prophet, said that Joseph frequented Palmyra to purchase newspapers or look for work, and attended the meetings of the "juvenile debating club," which met in the red schoolhouse on Durfee Street.[3]

Not long after the Smiths moved to the farm, "an unusual excitement [arose] on the subject of religion. It commenced with the Methodists, but soon became general among all the sects in that region of country. Indeed, the whole district of country seemed affected by it."[4] Churches proselytized, and large numbers of people joined the various denominations.[5]

Camp meetings were effective missionary programs, particularly for the Methodists, and were often held "on the edge of a grove of trees or in a small clearing in the midst of a forest."[6] Local settlers pitched their tents around the encampment,

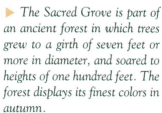

▶ *The Sacred Grove is part of an ancient forest in which trees grew to a girth of seven feet or more in diameter, and soared to heights of one hundred feet. The forest displays its finest colors in autumn.*

The predetermined spot in a grove of trees where Joseph chose to seclude himself for prayer was perhaps a clearing created by his father,[7] and was, for the young boy, a "silent grove."[8]

 (Opposite page) "After I had retired to the place where I had previously designed to go, having looked around me, and finding myself alone, I kneeled down and began to offer up the desires of my heart to God."[9]

The exact date of the first vision is not known. Although some have assumed that it occurred on April 6, 1820, the grove is quite barren at that time of year.

▶ *(Opposite page) Path through the Sacred Grove. "It was on the morning of a beautiful, clear day, early in the spring of eighteen hundred and twenty."*[10]

while farmers sold produce and liquor near camp. Meetings frequently lasted several days. Ministers rotated their presentations so that one was immediately followed by another, and occasionally two or three preached simultaneously in different parts of the camp. This constant fire of evangelism that prevailed in western New York, more than in any other part of the country, earned the region the title of "Burned-over District."

With such religious activity, young Joseph Smith became "seriously impressed with regard to the all-important concerns for the welfare of [his] immortal soul."[11] Described by his mother as a boy "less inclined to the perusal of books than any of the rest of our children, but far more given to meditation and deep study,"[12] Joseph learned from his observations of the world around him.

> I looked upon the sun, the glorious luminary of the earth, and also the moon, rolling in their majesty through the heavens, and also the stars shining in their courses . . . the earth upon which I stood . . . the beast of the field . . . the fowls of heaven . . . fish of the waters, and also man . . . [and] my heart exclaimed all these bear testimony and bespeak an omnipotent and omnipresent power, a being who maketh laws and decreeth, and bindeth all things in their bounds.[13]

While attending various religious meetings as often as time permitted, Joseph noticed that not only did the many sects not agree with each other on points of doctrine, but they also frequently harbored bitter feelings toward each other. Although he felt some desire to be united with the Methodist sect, he did not join any organized church, unlike his mother and three of his siblings—Samuel, Hyrum, and

Sophronia—all of whom joined the Presbyterian faith.[14] Instead he questioned, "What is to be done? Who of all these parties are right; or, are they all wrong together? If any one of them be right, which is it, and how shall I know it?"[15]

One day while reading in the Epistle of James, chapter one, verse five, he read: "If any of you lack wisdom, let him ask of God, that giveth to all men liberally, and upbraideth not; and it shall be given him."

Of all the profound scriptures found in the Bible, of all the powerful impressions they had left on the hearts of men throughout history, Joseph proclaimed, "Never did any passage of scripture come with more power to the heart of man than this did at this time to mine. It seemed to enter with great force into every feeling of my heart."[16] Although he had never, to that point, attempted to pray vocally for such an answer, the impact of James' message, combined with Joseph's simple childlike faith, convinced the youthful seeker that he must do as the scripture stated and personally "ask of God."

The exact day that he went into the grove of ancient trees in pursuit of his answer is not known, but in his 1838 history Joseph describes that morning as "a beautiful, clear day, early in the spring of eighteen hundred and twenty."[17]

Upon finding himself alone, young Joseph commenced offering up his heartfelt desires when he "was seized upon by some power which entirely overcame [him], and had such astonishing influence over [him] as to bind [his] tongue so that [he] could not speak."[18] Joseph continued, "I heard a noise behind me like some one walking towards me . . . the noise of walking seemed to draw nearer, I sprang upon my feet and looked round, but saw no person or thing."[19]

After that, "thick darkness gathered around me, and it seemed to me for a time as if I were doomed to sudden destruction. But, exerting all my powers to call upon God to deliver me out of the power of this enemy which had seized upon me, and at the very moment when I was ready to sink into despair and abandon myself to destruction . . . just at this moment of great alarm, I saw a pillar of light exactly over my head, above the brightness of the sun, which descended gradually until it fell upon me,"[20] and "filled me with unspeakable joy."[21] To Joseph, the light was like a "pillar of fire"[22] which, when it reached the tops of the trees, illuminated the surrounding forest in a glorious and brilliant manner, as though it would consume the leaves by fire.[23]

When the light rested upon Joseph, he saw two personages, "whose brightness and glory defy all description,"[24] and "who exactly resembled each other in features, and likeness, surrounded with a brilliant light which eclipsed the sun at noon-day."[25] One of the personages, calling Joseph by name and pointing to the other personage, said, "This is my beloved Son, Hear him."[26]

After Joseph had composed himself, he addressed the personage to whom he was directed and asked which sect he should join. He was told to "go not after them," for "all religious denominations

(Opposite page) "My father, who was laboring along with me, discovered something to be wrong with me, and told me to go home. I started with the intention of going to the house; but, in attempting to cross the fence out of the field where we were, my strength entirely failed me, and I fell helpless on the ground . . ."[27]

Path to Sacred Grove in winter. The winters of western New York are long and cold. Only a few summer months are exempt from the possibility of snow.

were believing in incorrect doctrines, and that none of them was acknowledged of God as His church and Kingdom."[28] This glorious being, who identified Himself as He who "was crucified for the world that all those who believe on my name may have Eternal life," continued, saying, "My son, thy sins are forgiven thee. Go thy way, walk in my statutes, and keep my commandments."[29] During the vision, Joseph learned many other things, "which [he could] not write at this time,"[30] but was promised "that the fulness of the gospel should at some future time be made known unto [him]."[31] We also know that angels attended this magnificent event.[32]

Following this vision, Joseph had an understanding unmatched by any other person on the earth. By firsthand experience he had learned about deity. He knew that God, the Father, and God, the Son, were two distinct beings and that they looked exactly alike. He had seen their interaction with each other. They had called him by name; they knew him personally and they knew his concerns. He had gained an understanding of their love for mankind as well as a glimpse of the work they would perform to save humanity. He now knew that they did not intend for men to create their own doctrines or philosophies about salvation. The impact of this vision on Joseph was exhilarating, for he stated, "My soul was filled with love and for many days I could rejoice with great joy and the Lord was with me."[33]

After leaving the grove, Joseph returned to the family cabin, whereupon entering, he leaned against the fireplace. His mother, apparently noticing a change in his countenance, inquired as to his condition. Joseph replied, "Never mind, all is well—I am well enough off."[34] Joseph told his family of his experience, and they soon came to believe him and were willing to sacrifice everything they had in order to stand by his account. His reception in the community, however, was quite different.

A few days after the vision, when Joseph shared an account of the vision with a Methodist minister, the preacher not only treated the vision with contempt, but stated that it "was all of the devil."[35] That one conversation was spread amongst all of the village clergy until *all* of the sects were united, said Joseph, "to excite the public mind against me, and create a bitter persecution."[36]

Only Joseph had been in the grove during the vision, and the fourteen-year-old boy would have to stand alone in his assertions. Nevertheless, the reality of it was enough to fortify him for, said he, "I had seen a vision; I knew it, and I knew that God knew it, and I could not deny it."[37]

"This marvelous theophany," said President Gordon B. Hinckley, "[was] unequaled since the events on the Mount of Transfiguration two millennia ago."[38] Joseph's vision of God the Father and His Son Jesus Christ initiated the opening of a new dispensation, or "fulness of times," a time in which "all things" would be gathered together in Christ (Ephesians 1:10; Acts 3:21).

 (Opposite page) "I saw a pillar of light exactly over my head, above the brightness of the sun, which descended gradually until it fell upon me."[39]

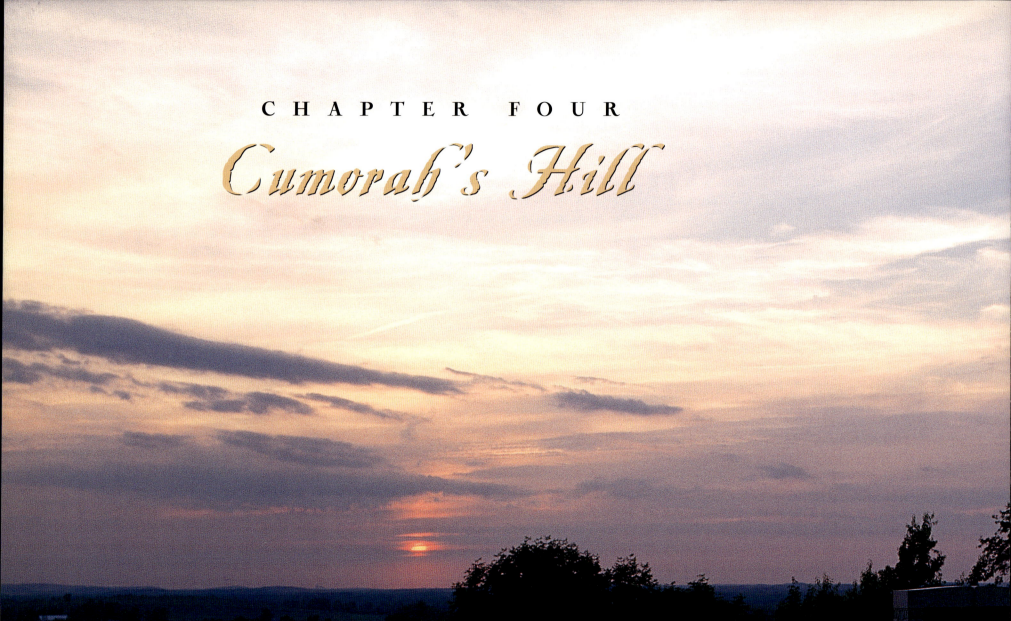

CHAPTER FOUR

Cumorah's Hill

"... a vision came to Joseph's mind in which he saw, and knew, the place where the plates were buried."

JOSEPH SMITH HISTORY

Monument on the Hill Cumorah at sunset.

he reality and importance of Joseph's vision did not eliminate the need for the Smiths to perform their daily labor. But the task of making their home was now more difficult as Joseph found that his "telling the story had excited a great deal of prejudice against [him] . . . and was the cause of great persecution, which continued to increase."[1]

Nevertheless, the family managed to clear and fence sixty acres and sell wheat to grain dealers.[2] They also began construction of a frame house in November 1822. Alvin, the oldest of the Smith boys, desired "a nice, pleasant room for Father and Mother to sit in and everything arranged for their comfort, [that] they [should] not work anymore as they have done."[3]

The day of 21 September 1823, the fall equinox, found the Smith boys helping their father with the harvest during the day, followed by a family discussion of the diversity of churches that night.[4] Joseph was in an unusually thoughtful mood, feeling the guilt of foolish errors—not of serious sins but an inconsistency with that which ought to be maintained by someone "who was called of God as I had been."[5] Having a desire "to be prepared in heart to commune with some kind of messenger who could communicate to him the desired information of his acceptance with God," Joseph prayed long into the night while the others were fast asleep.[6] At some time, deep in the night, the loft of the cabin where the boys slept was filled with brilliant light, and a glorious personage, an angel, appeared at Joseph's bedside, standing in the air. The young man's initial fears soon fled as the messenger called him by name and announced that he was a messenger from God and that his name was Moroni.

The angel stated that God had a work for Joseph to do. In a profound prophecy, to a relatively unknown boy in a humble cabin, Moroni proclaimed that "[Joseph's] name should be had for good and evil among all nations, kindreds, and tongues, or that it should be both good and evil spoken of among all people."[7] Moroni then informed Joseph of a book written on plates of gold, which gave an account of the former inhabitants of the American continent. The fulness of the gospel, as given to them by the Savior, was recorded on the plates by ancient prophets. Moroni was the last to write on the golden record. Deposited with the plates were stones in silver bows, known as the Urim and Thummim, which were prepared for the translation of the record. The heavenly messenger then proceeded to recite, with a few variations, passages from the Bible pertaining to such topics as the last days, temples, priesthood, families, the millennium, the gathering of Israel, and the coming of Elijah the prophet, as found in the Bible. Other scriptures were also expounded, and a vision came to Joseph's mind in which he saw, and knew, the place where the plates were buried.[8]

Having given his message, the light gathered around the angel and he left the room. Twice more during the same evening, Moroni reappeared to Joseph and repeated the same message while adding further prophecies concerning the world in the last days, and warning Joseph that Satan would try to tempt the young man to get the plates for the purpose of obtaining riches. At the conclusion of Moroni's third visit, the cock announced the morning with his crowing. Joseph had not slept at all.

In the fields the next day, Joseph Sr. noticed his son's fatigue and sent him back to the house. On his

▲ *Eight witnesses. One of four bronze bas reliefs on the monument at the top of the Hill Cumorah.*

◀ *(Opposite page) "We are not erecting (the monument) to perpetuate the deeds of Moroni . . . we humbly pray unto thee that it may be preserved . . . as a testimony of God, of Jesus Christ, and of the dealing of Jesus Christ with the people that lived anciently upon this continent."[9]*

way home, Joseph received a fourth visit from Moroni, who repeated the message of the previous night and told Joseph to return and tell his father what had happened. Joseph Sr. recognized that these manifestations were of God, and told Joseph to go, as directed, to the hill where the plates were buried.[10]

Situated four miles south of Palmyra village, the hill would have been known to most residents in the area because the major highway heading south, Canandaigua Road, skirted along its west side. Joseph Smith described the hill as "convenient to the village of Manchester, Ontario county, New York, . . . of considerable size, and the most elevated of any in the neighborhood."[11] The hill had "a varied appearance: the north end rose suddenly from the plain, forming a promontory without timber, but covered with grass. As you passed to the south you soon came to scattering timber, the surface having been cleared by art or by wind. . . . The part cleared was only occupied for pasturage, its steep ascent and narrow summit not admitting the plow of the husbandman, with any degree of ease or profit. . . . There were several trees standing; enough to cause a shade in summer, but not so much as to prevent the surface being covered with grass which was also the case when the record was first found.[12]

We don't know when the hill became known as "Cumorah." Joseph rarely called the hill "Cumorah,"[13] but simply referred to it as "the place where the plates were deposited."[14] In recording one revelation, he wrote, "Glad tidings from Cumorah" (Doctrine and Covenants 128:20). The Book of Mormon refers to "the land of Cumorah, by a hill which was called Cumorah" (Mormon 6:2), the location where an ancient American nation, the

Nephites, went to battle, and were defeated and destroyed. By at least 1835, the hill was known as "Cumorah" by those associated with the Church.[15]

On 22 September 1823, Joseph followed Moroni's instructions and walked the three miles to the hill where the plates were deposited. Along the way, he felt the influence of two distinct but invisible powers—one that caused him to ponder on the mercy of the Lord and the need to obey His instructions, and another power, which brought ideas of aggrandizement and wealth.[16] Upon arriving at the place, "on the west side of this hill, not far from the top," which he had seen in the vision, Joseph found a stone, "thick and rounding in the middle on the upper side, and thinner towards the edges," of which only the middle was above ground. Clearing the dirt and finding a lever, he removed the stone.[17]

We can only imagine the awe he must have felt as he beheld the contents of this box, which had apparently been created "by laying stones together in some kind of cement."[18] Inside he saw the gold plates, two stones in a silver bow—the Urim and Thummim—and a breastplate.[19] Joseph tried to remove the plates, but an unseen power sent a shock through him. Weakened, he attempted twice more to remove the plates, resulting in two successively stronger shocks. "Why can I not obtain this book?" he asked, frustrated.

◀ *(Opposite page) This cement replica of the Book of Mormon at the base of the Hill Cumorah documents the promise given to all seekers of truth as quoted in Moroni, chapter 10, verse 4. ". . . and if ye shall ask with a sincere heart, with real intent, having faith in Christ, he will manifest the truth of it unto you by the power of the Holy Ghost."*

CUMORAH AS A DRUMLIN

The Hill Cumorah owes its unusual shape to the fact that most of the land that comprises present-day New York was at one time covered with ancient glaciers. Flowing ice from these glaciers deposited debris into "elongated half-egg shaped forms, the most symmetrical of which are called drumlins."[1] Hundreds of these narrow hills, oriented in a north-south direction, are found in New York, and nowhere in the world are they better developed than they are around the Palmyra region. The Hill Cumorah is a typical drumlin, with its south sides rising gradually up to a fairly level, yet narrow top, while the east, west, and north slopes drop off sharply.

1. John. H. Thompson, *Geography of New York, State* (Syracuse, New York: Syracuse University Press, 1966), 20.

Assuming he was alone, Joseph was astonished at the response, "Because you have not kept the commandments of the Lord."[20] At this, he looked up and saw Moroni again, and realized that he had "failed to remember the great end for which [the plates] had been kept, and in consequence could not have power to take them."[21]

Joseph began to pray and received a vision of the "prince of darkness" and his hosts, so he would "know hereafter the two powers and never be influ-

enced or overcome by that wicked one."[22] This left an impression on him throughout the rest of his life, so that he was always "willing to keep the commandments of God."[23] Other instructions were given and Joseph was commanded to return to Cumorah each year on September 22 until he could receive the plates.[24] Admonished to "Forget not to pray," Joseph then returned home.[25]

The following September, Joseph fully expected to be able to retrieve the plates. On the specified day, he returned to the hill, removed the stone lid, and physically lifted the plates out of the box. With a fleeting thought that perhaps some other valuable object might be in the container as well, Joseph laid the plates down to look inside. Seeing nothing, he replaced the stone and turned to pick up the plates, but they were gone. Once again, he turned to the Lord in prayer, and once again Moroni appeared and informed Joseph that he had disobeyed a commandment by laying the plates down.[26] The young prophet had yet to learn the great care required to guard this sacred ancient record, so dearly valued by prophets of old (see Enos 1:16).

Joseph was once again allowed to look under the stone to view the plates, but when he tried to retrieve them, a force threw him to the ground. Upon recovery, he found himself alone once again and returned to his house in grief.[27]

Little is recorded of Joseph's visits to the hill the following two years. Before September 1826, Joseph had been living in Colesville, working for Josiah Stowell; he had to travel nearly 150 miles to Manchester to keep his appointments at Cumorah. During this time period, Hyrum married Jerusha, and Joseph made plans to marry Emma Hale. Early

DAVID WHITMER AND MORONI

David Whitmer may have been one of the first to note the unusual name of "Cumorah" as he was transporting Joseph and Oliver to Fayette in 1829. He later recounted:

When I was returning to Fayette with Joseph and Oliver all of us riding in the wagon . . . a very pleasant, nice-looking old man suddenly appeared by the side of our wagon who saluted us with "Good morning, it is very warm," at the same time wiping his face or forehead with his hand. We returned the salutation, and by a sign from Joseph I invited him to ride, if he was going our way. But he said very pleasantly, "No, I am going to Cumorah." This name was something new to me, I did not know what Cumorah meant. We all gazed at him and at each other, and as I looked around inquiringly of Joseph, the old man instantly disappeared, so that I did not see him again.[1]

David understood from Joseph that the old man was most likely Moroni, the messenger to whom Joseph had given the gold plates upon completing their translation, and prior to his departure from Harmony.[2]

1. David Whitmer, "Report of Elders Orson Pratt and Joseph F. Smith," *Deseret Evening News*, Salt Lake City, 16 November 1878. As quoted in Larry C. Porter, "Organizational Origins of the Church of Jesus Christ, 6 April 1830" in *Regional Studies in Latter-day Saint Church History/ New York.* Eds. Larry C. Porter, Milton V. Backman Jr. and Susan Easton Black (Provo, Utah: Dept. of Church History and Doctrine, Brigham Young University, 1992), 208.

2. Richard L. Bushman, *Joseph Smith and the Beginnings of Mormonism* (Urbana and Chicago: University of Illinois Press, 1988), 103.

"*On the west side of this hill, not far from the top, under a stone of considerable size, lay the plates, deposited in a stone box.*"[28]

❧

▼ *Joseph receiving instruction from the angel Moroni. One of the four bronze bas reliefs on the monument at the top of the Hill Cumorah.*

45

in 1827, Joseph and his new bride, Emma, moved in with Joseph's family.

Some time before September 22, 1827 an errand took Joseph to the village of Manchester. Late in the night, long after the hour when he was expected, Joseph entered the house in an exhausted state. When questioned by his father, Joseph replied, "I have taken the severest chastisement that I have ever had in my life."[29] Passing Cumorah on his way home, the angel Moroni appeared to him, telling Joseph that he needed to be more engaged in the work of the Lord and the time had come to retrieve the plates. "I now know the course that I am to pursue, so all will be well," he reassured his parents.[30]

This four-year period from 1823 to 1827 was truly a condensed course of spiritual education for the Prophet as he matured in knowledge and stature. During these years, plus the two years following, records indicate that he had at least twenty-two separate interviews with Moroni,[31] but many other angels appeared as well. "[I] received many visits from the angels of God, unfolding the majesty and glory of the events that should transpire in the last days," Joseph said.[32] About sixty heavenly personages appeared to Joseph during his life.[33] Even though his temporal education was sparse, in respect to spiritual matters he was the finest student learning from the greatest instructors.

As the date approached for Joseph to receive the plates from Moroni, Joseph Knight and Josiah Stowell, two trusted friends from the Colesville region, arrived in Manchester on a business trip and stayed at the Smith home for a few days. It is not likely that their timing was a coincidence, since both of them knew of the coming forth of the record.

On the evening of September 22, 1827, Emma apparently accompanied her new husband to the hill, and remained at the base of the hill in prayer while Joseph went to retrieve the record.[34] Her role this night appears to foreshadow much that she would experience over the next seventeen years of marriage with Joseph. Patiently she would wait for him to perform his duties, while she—not being a participant in most of the manifestations—faithfully supported her husband, the Prophet. For her, duty would never be convenient. Over the years, she would wait for Joseph to return from missions, to be released from unjust imprisonments, to return from caring over the Church, and much more. All the while she would stand by—patiently, prayerfully, and faithfully.

When morning arrived and Joseph and Emma had not yet returned to the house, Lucy began to be concerned. At last Joseph entered the house, but his mother did not see any sign of the plates. Sensing his mother's fears, Joseph took her into another room and showed her something that he had brought from the hill: the Urim and Thummim, "two smooth three-cornered diamonds set in glass . . . set in silver bows, which were connected with each other in much the same way as old fashioned spectacles." Joseph referred to them as "a key"[35] and explained that after receiving the plates, instead of taking them back to the house, he had found a place to seclude them for safety. The plates may even have been hidden somewhere near the hill itself, as Lucy indicated in her history:

"Finding an old birch log much decayed, excepting the bark, which was in a measure sound, [Joseph] took his pocket knife and cut the bark with some care, then turned it back, and made a hole of sufficient size

▲ *Three witnesses. One of the four bronze bas reliefs on the monument at the top of the Hill Cumorah.*

◀ *(Opposite page) It is both significant and symbolic that in the dark of night Joseph retrieved the gold plates that would bring spiritual light to the earth.*

▲ *A stand of birch trees similar to where Joseph may have secreted the plates inside the trunk of a fallen birch.*

▶ *(Opposite page) Today, hundreds of participants, many living in tents and trailers north of the hill, work long, hot hours in late June preparing for the pageant. Beginning in July, tens of thousands of visitors worldwide are treated to the largest outdoor pageant in America—on the hill where the gold plates once lay hidden.*

to receive the plates, and laying them in the cavity thus formed, he replaced the bark after which he laid across the log, in several places, some old stuff that happened to lay near."[36]

The following day, Joseph went to Macedon to earn money so he could construct a box to hold the plates. When Joseph Sr. learned that a mob was gathering with the intent of finding the plates, he sent Emma to Macedon in order to inform Joseph Jr. Using the Urim and Thummim, which he kept on his person at all times, Joseph determined that the plates were safe; however, he returned home with Emma to retrieve them from their hiding place.

As Joseph took them from their hiding place and started home, he was met by three attackers. Joseph knocked each of the three down with his right fist, dislocating his right thumb in the process. He ran three miles with the fifty-pound plates under his left arm until he arrived home, "speechless from fright and the fatigue of running."[37] Joseph Sr., Joseph Knight, and Josiah Stowell were sent in pursuit of the assailants, who had already fled.

Over the next few months, many groups attempted to get the plates, trespassing on the Smith property to search for them. Joseph repeatedly moved them from place to place to avoid their being found. He remembered Moroni's earlier warning when he delivered the plates:

> Now you have got the Record into your own hands, and you are but a man, therefore you will have to be watchful and faithful to your trust, or you will be overpowered by wicked men, for they will lay every plan and scheme that is possible to get it away from you, and if you do not take heed continually, they will succeed. While it was in my hands, I could keep it, and no man had power to take it away; but now I give it up to you. Beware, and look well to your ways, and you shall have power to retain it, until the time for it to be translated.[38]

Although many of Joseph's critics claimed not to believe in the reality of the gold plates, numerous attempts were made to find them nonetheless; and for many years Cumorah was referred to as "Mormon Hill," "Golden Bible Hill," and "Bible Hill."[39] From time to time, Church members wanting to visit the hill were driven away by those who lived nearby.[40]

Eventually, the Church was able to purchase the lower part of the hill. The purchase of the rest of the hill, however, was difficult because the owner, Mr.

Pliney T. Sexton, a Palmyra banker, was determined to sell the land for far more than its worth. After Sexton's death, however, his heirs, wanting their money from the estate, sold the rest of the Hill Cumorah to the Church in 1928, along with adjacent farms.[41] Now the Church could start the plans to erect a monument on the top of the hill.

On 21 July 1935, President Grant dedicated the forty-foot shaft of Vermont granite, which stands on the hill where Joseph had his annual visits with the angel. The monument symbolizes a "pillar of light," with a four-sided base depicting events associated with the golden plates, and the top crowned with a ten-foot-tall bronze statue of Moroni.[42] In the dedicatory prayer, President Grant said, "We are not erecting [the monument] to perpetuate the deeds of Moroni, nor are we erecting it to honor his father Mormon, nor indeed to perpetuate the life and deeds of Joseph Smith . . . we humbly pray unto thee that it may be preserved . . . as a testimony of God, of Jesus Christ, and of the dealing of Jesus Christ with the people that lived anciently upon this continent."[43]

In 1936, Oliver R. Smith, a missionary who had trained in speech and theater, wrote a pageant, "Truth From the Earth," which was performed on the flats below Cumorah, while the audience sat on the hill. A new script was written the following year, and the production, named "America's Witness for Christ," was staged on the hill while the audience watched from below. The show became an annual event, with the exception of the years 1942-1947, during World War II. The Hill Cumorah Pageant has been modified over the years, most recently in 1988,[44] however, its purpose has remained constant: to teach the world about "Another Testament of Jesus Christ."

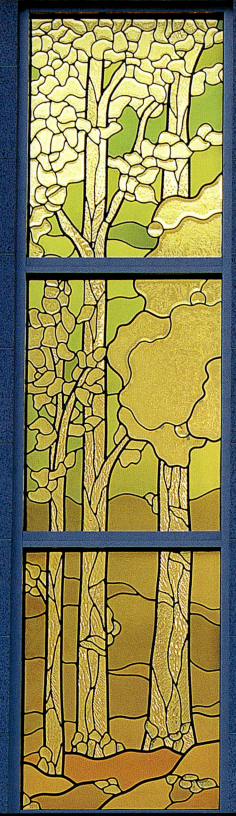

> "I regard this [Palmyra] temple as perhaps the most significant, in one respect, in the entire Church. It was right here in the Sacred Grove where it all began."
>
> PRESIDENT GORDON B. HINCKLEY

Light shining through stained glass windows depicting the Sacred Grove in the Palmyra Temple. The temple was dedicated April 6, 2000—the 170th anniversary of the organization of the Church of Jesus Christ of Latter-day Saints.

CHAPTER FIVE

Sacred Places

▲ In November of 1823, Alvin Smith became ill and was administered a large dose of a mercurous chloride cathartic by a doctor who was not the regular family physician. The mass lodged in Alvin's intestines, causing gangrene and eventually death. Because Alvin had shown the greatest zeal towards the record of the Nephites, the family could not bear to hear about the plates for some time after his death.

▶ (Opposite page) Kitchen at the Smith log cabin.

Despite relentless persecution, the Smith family spent many pleasant hours listening to Joseph describe what he was learning. Lucy Mack Smith describes the evenings spent at home

> . . . all seated in a circle, father, mother, sons, and daughters, and giving the most profound attention to a boy, eighteen years of age, who had never read the Bible through in his life. . . . During our evening conversations, Joseph would occasionally give us some of the most amusing recitals that could be imagined. He would describe the ancient inhabitants of this continent, their dress, mode of travelling, and the animals upon which they rode . . . This he would do with as much ease, seemingly, as if he had spent his whole life with them.[1]

These events solidified the family's conviction that Joseph spoke the truth. "We were now confirmed in the opinion that God was about to bring to light something upon which we could stay our minds, or that would give us a more perfect knowledge . . . the sweetest union and happiness pervaded our house."[2]

In November 1823, barely two months after Moroni's first visit, Joseph's oldest brother, Alvin, became ill with bilious colic and was administered a large dose of calomel, a mercurous chloride cathartic, by a physician. The solidified mass of powder lodged in his digestive system, causing gangrene and his eventual death on 19 November 1823. In his last hours, Alvin instructed Hyrum, "I have done all I could to make our dear parents comfortable. I want you to go on and finish the house, and take care of them in their old age, and do not any more let them work hard, as they are now in old age."[3] Describing Alvin, Joseph later stated, "He was one of the noblest of the sons of men . . . In him there was no guile."[4]

Because Alvin had manifested the greatest zeal regarding the record on the plates, it was some time before the family could again bear to hear about them. Eventually recovering from their mourning, the family also resumed building their house, although at a slower pace.

Persecution persisted, not just toward Joseph Jr. but toward the family as well. In September of 1824, rumors arose that Alvin Smith's body had been exhumed from the Palmyra cemetery and mutilated. Joseph Sr. and some neighbors had to dig up the grave and examine the body in order to dispel the rumors. Joseph Sr.'s pain-filled reprimand towards those who would even start such a rumor was printed in the local newspaper, the *Wayne Sentinel*.[5]

Eventually, the family hired a neighbor, Russell Stoddard, to finish the house, and greater responsibility fell upon Joseph Jr. and Hyrum to bring in more income. Nevertheless, Father and Mother Smith must have rejoiced as they left the little cabin and moved into their new frame house, possibly as early as the spring of 1825, a few months before its completion.[6]

By the end of November of 1825, prospects appeared bright for the Smith household. The new home was completed, and only one more payment was due on the farm. Furthermore, Josiah Stowell and Joseph Knight had offered to pay the Smiths in advance for a quantity of flour to be delivered the ensuing fall. Joseph Sr. only needed to go to Colesville to obtain the money. As he and young Joseph were leaving on this journey, Father Smith instructed Hyrum to visit the agent in Canandaigua and inform him that the payment would be delivered by Christmas Day.[7]

During their absence, Mr. Stoddard, the carpenter they had hired, and two other men approached the house. Undeterred by the Smith family's previous refusals to sell him the house and land, Stoddard and two assistants had raised enough money to purchase the farm outright. They then approached the land agent with a fabricated story that Josephs Sr. and Jr. had run off and that Hyrum was "doing all manner of mischief to the farm."[8] The agent accepted their story and money and gave Stoddard and his partners the deed to the farm. With this paper in hand, they first approached Lucy Smith, then Hyrum, saying, "we have bought the place, and paid for it, and we now

◀ *The back room in the loft of the cabin would have been used by the Smith daughters.*
▶ *(Opposite page) The rebuilt Smith log cabin.*

forbid your touching anything on the farm; and we also warn you to leave forthwith, and give possession to the lawful owners."[9]

Later, upon learning the truth of the situation, the agent was "highly enraged" and forced the three to return to his office by threat of warrant. The trio agreed to return the deed only if the Smiths could raise $1,000, ten times the amount the Smiths owed with the last payment, by ten o'clock two days later. Lucy said, "The anxiety of mind that I suffered that day can more easily be imagined than described."[10] Even though Joseph Sr. returned from his trip in time to help direct a frantic search to raise the money, the best they could do was to arrange for another, more sympathetic buyer for the farm. The Smiths lost the farm, but Lemuel Durfee, the new owner, allowed them to rent the frame house for the next four years. During this time, many significant and sacred events would transpire, including Joseph and Emma's marriage, and Joseph obtaining the gold plates.

In the spring of 1829 the Smith family was forced to move back into the small log cabin they had left; but by then Hyrum and his wife, Jerusha Barden, occupied the small edifice and were expecting their second child. Now eleven people filled the rooms.[11]

For the next two years, until the fall of 1830, this undersized cabin also accommodated countless others who were brought to this small but hallowed spot. Many gathered at the Smiths' "snug log-house" in Manchester for shelter and instruction. Joseph preached there several times to crowds that filled the cabin to capacity. Parley P. Pratt, a future apostle of the Church, described such a gathering as his first introduction to the prophet, which just happened to be on a day when "the two large rooms were filled with attentive listeners, and [Joseph] invited me [Parley] to preach. . . . We repaired from the meeting to the water's edge, and at his request, I baptized several persons.[12]

However, the persecution toward the Smiths accelerated, and Lucy stated that due to the animosity of many of their neighbors "and ten thousand discouragements it is not probable that we shall locate in these parts again."[13] Even so, she appeared to be at peace, for she went on to say in a letter to her sister-in-law, dated January 24 of that year, that "never before have I been . . . more content with my lot, having obtained a token of his grace."[14]

(Opposite page) "While I was thus in the act of calling upon God, I discovered a light appearing in my room . . . when immediately a personage appeared at my bedside."[15] None of the other Smith boys awakened from their sleep as Moroni appeared to Joseph.

The back of the rebuilt Smith log cabin demonstrates the slab-sawn room that was added in order to relieve the cramped quarters. In spite of its small size, many significant events of the restoration are associated with this cabin.

JOSEPH SR. IMPRISONED

The Smith family was preparing to leave Palmyra when a man arrived at the door of the Smith home with a fourteen-dollar note, which he held against Joseph Sr. The man offered to forgive the debt if Smith would burn some copies of the Book of Mormon, then called a constable when the Prophet's father refused. An offer to pay with Lucy's gold beads was rejected, and Joseph Sr. was taken to Canandaigua, where he was thrown in the dungeon; his cell mate was a convicted murderer.

Joseph Sr. said: "I shuddered when I first heard these heavy doors creaking upon their hinges; but then, I thought to myself, I was not the first man who had been imprisoned for the truth's sake; and when I should meet Paul in the Paradise of God, I could tell him that I, too, had been in bonds for the Gospel which he had preached." Four days later he was allowed to move to the jail yard where he remained for thirty days, and where "he preached during his confinement here every Sunday. . . . When he was released he baptized two persons whom he had thus converted."[1]

With Hyrum and his family already gone to Colesville, Lucy was alone with her youngest daughter while Joseph Sr. was imprisoned, and a mob, intent on ransacking the cabin, was finally dispersed at the timely return of her son William.

1. Lucy Smith, *Biographical Sketches of Joseph Smith the Prophet and His Progenitors for Many Generations* (Independence, Missouri: Herald Publishing House, 1969), 159-164.

In September of 1830, the family prepared to move to Seneca County, to a small community located between the villages of Waterloo and Seneca Falls, called "Kingdom" (although, in her history, Lucy Smith calls it "Waterloo"[16]).

The responsibility of moving the family fell to Samuel, who had just returned from a mission and was trying to recover from illness. But, said Lucy, "after much fatigue and perplexities of various kinds, he succeeded in getting us [to Waterloo]."[17]

After the Smiths moved away, their former home was used as a barn and fell into disrepair before coming down completely. The foundation was covered with soil,[18] and for years people were unsure of its exact location. With time and research, the foundation was finally located and rebuilt as close to the original Smith cabin as possible. President Gordon B. Hinckley dedicated the reconstructed cabin on 22 March 1998, saying, "This place will always be a sacred place. I hope that it will bring alive many memories of the past, rich and wonderful, and there will come into the heart of each one who comes here a quickening of testimony concerning this great and latter-day work."[19]

The reconstructed small log cabin would not be the last "sacred place" built in this area. On 6 April 2000, the morning rain that had been falling on the former Joseph Smith Sr. farm subsided. On a small hill overlooking the rain-soaked Sacred Grove, log cabin, and frame house stood a new building. Made with marbled granite to glisten in the light, this building was the Palmyra Temple. On that day, the 170th anniversary of the organization of The Church of Jesus Christ of Latter-day Saints, the holy edifice was

▶ *(Opposite page) Three sacred places . . . a temple, a cabin, and a grove.*

KINGDOM

Joseph Smith Sr. and his wife, Lucy, driven from the Palmyra region by the animosity of the citizens and the loss of their farm, moved to a location in Seneca County during the fall of 1830. This area was called "Waterloo" by Lucy in her history, but was actually the small community of Kingdom located between the villages of Waterloo and Seneca Falls.[1] Shortly after arriving in this community, the Smith family was "made to realize that the hearts of the people were in the hands of the Lord; for we had scarcely unpacked our goods, when one of our new neighbors, a Mr. Osgood, came in and invited us to drive our stock and teams to his barn-yard, and feed them from his barn, free of cost, until we could make further arrangements."[2] Others also arrived to welcome them. The tavern keeper's wife made "delicate eatables," and kindness was shown to them "day

by day," which prompted in the Smiths "the liveliest sensations of gratitude."[3] Upon learning that the Smith family held devotions each evening with singing and prayers, their rented home soon became a gathering place each night for "some dozen or twenty persons."[4]

Ironically, this place that accepted the Smiths with kindness and love had originally been named "Devil's Kingdom," due to its reputation for being the "toughest spot on the Buffalo turnpike." Here, gangsters, fighters, and adventurers gathered for cockfights, fox chases, wrestling matches, prize fights, and horse races. Because of its location along the turnpike, and subsequently along the Seneca Canal, Kingdom became a frequent stopping place for stagecoaches as well as canal boats. Like the "publicans and sinners" who often gave the greatest heed to Jesus, so the people of a lesser reputation in New York gave the kindest response to the family of a prophet (Matthew 11:19).

After the revelation to gather in Ohio was received in the spring of 1831, the saints in Seneca County, about eighty in number, gathered at the river to set forth to Zion by boat, while "the people of the surrounding country came and bade us farewell, invoking the blessing of heaven upon our heads."[5]

Today, the village of Kingdom no longer exists. The only indicator of its former location is a New York State historical marker for the "Kingdom Cemetery" on the north side of Highway 5, about one mile west of the town of Seneca Falls.

1. Larry C. Porter, "A Study of the Origins of the Church of Jesus Christ of Latter-day Saints in the States of New York and Pennsylvania, 1816-1831" (Ph.D. dissertation, Brigham Young University, 1971), 269.

2. Lucy Smith, *Biographical Sketches of Joseph Smith the Prophet and His Progenitors for Many Generations* (Independence, Missouri: Herald Publishing House, 1969), 173.

3. Ibid, 167-168.

4. Ibid.

5. Porter, "Origins," 270-271.

◁ *(Opposite page) The Palmyra Temple.*

 Stained glass windows on the Palmyra Temple. "The stained glass windows representing the Sacred Grove brought to my mind the statement in the Doctrine and Covenants [124:26] where the Lord said, 'Send ye swift messengers, yea, chosen messengers, and say unto them: Come ye, with all your gold, and your silver, and your precious stones, and with all your antiquities; and with all who have knowledge of antiquities, that will come, may come, and bring the box-tree and the fir-tree, and the pine-tree, together with all the precious trees of the earth.'"[20] (President Boyd K. Packer at the temple dedication.)

dedicated to the Lord. In the dedicatory prayer, President Hinckley stated: "But it was here, on this land which the Smiths once farmed, it was here in the Grove below and to the west that Thou, the Almighty God of the universe, and Thy Beloved Son, the resurrected Lord, appeared to the boy Joseph Smith. This wondrous event parted the curtain that had been closed for centuries. This marvelous appearance, which is the foundation of Thy work in this dispensation, brought back to earth a knowledge of the one true God and the resurrected Lord."[21]

One year earlier at the groundbreaking ceremony for this same temple, he had stated, "I regard this temple as perhaps the most significant, in one respect, in the entire Church. It was right here in the Sacred Grove where it all began."[22]

To Latter-day Saints, the most significant blessings are those received in the holy temples and pertain to sealing of families for eternity. How very appropriate then, that on the same land where God the Father and His Holy Son Jesus Christ appeared to open a new dispensation, a temple would be built where the blessings of that dispensation could be received to the fullest. Today these sacred places—a cabin, a house, and a temple—remain on the land where "a restoration of all things" began, standing as witnesses to the world that God communicates once again with His children on earth.

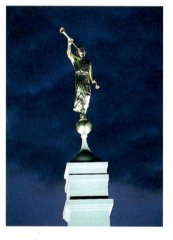

"There is this sense, as patrons drive up the hill, that they are ascending to something loftier. From certain points in the distance, the temple appears to be hovering over the area."[23] (Dave Richards, local architect for the temple.)

CHAPTER SIX

Susquehanna and the Great Bend

Even today vistas of the valley are limited due to the thick foliage, and one feels a sense of isolation from the outer world while traveling through this narrow pass.

The Susquehanna River banks are graced with beautiful green ferns and richly hued grasses.

(Opposite page) The misty Susquehanna River at Harmony, Pennsylvania. "The voice of Michael on the banks of the Susquehanna, detecting the devil when he appeared as an angel of light!" (D&C 128:19)

The name "Susquehanna" is an Indian name. Hanna signifies "a stream of water," and susque is generally believed to mean "crooked."[1]

Almost hidden in the northeast corner of Pennsylvania lies a valley, "unsurpassed for the beauty of its scenery."[2] Created by a diversion of the Susquehanna River from its New York course by sweeping south around a spur of the Allegheny and the Oauquaga Mountains, the area became known as the "Great Bend." The Susquehanna River flows through this picturesque twenty-mile valley before returning to New York to continue its long trek to the Atlantic Ocean. Even today, vistas of the valley are limited due to the thick foliage, and one feels a sense of isolation from the outer world while traveling through this narrow pass.

This area was described as "exceedingly broken and hilly, the Oauquaga Mountains occupying so large a part as to leave but very little level land north of the Susquehanna River. . . . Only by dint of commendable perseverance and toil has any of the land been improved, except, possibly, a little that lies along the river and near the beds of the few small streams."[3]

Isaac Hale first went down the Susquehanna River to the Great Bend in 1787. "After exploring the county, and getting acquainted with the older settlers," he returned to Vermont, where he married Elizabeth Lewis.[4] He and his brother-in-law Nathaniel Lewis and their wives then traveled two hundred miles, in carts pulled by steers, to the township of Harmony.

In 1853, a new township, Oakland, was created from Harmony township, and although the Smith and Hale homes are presently located in Oakland, the location is referred to as "Harmony" throughout this chapter, to be consistent with Joseph's historical record.

Over the years, Hale purchased large tracts of land and became quite well respected in the community. He was a man of "forethought and generosity" as he often shared his good[s] with others.[5] His wife, Elizabeth, was a faithful member of the Methodist church for fifty years, and an acquaintance said of her, "I never visited her but I thought I had learned something useful."[6] Together they had nine children. On 10 July 1804, their seventh child was born; they named her Emma.

In October of 1825, Joseph Smith arrived in Harmony for the first time. He had been hired by Josiah Stowell, of South Bainbridge (Afton), New

 Site of the Hale home foundation. The Hales' land was included in the Harmony township, but it was not part of Harmony village, which was situated one and a half miles east of the Hale home and across the river.

▶ *(Opposite page) Rocks along the shore of Susquehanna River. As a break from the tedious work of translation, Joseph and Oliver would sometimes go down to the river to throw rocks into the water.*

York to help search and dig for some purported lost Spanish silver mines that were supposedly located near the Hale homestead.[7] Josiah had heard through a relative that Joseph "possessed certain keys, by which he could discern things invisible to the natural eye,"[8] but after searching unsuccessfully for a month, Joseph convinced the elderly man to quit digging.[9] During this time, Joseph boarded at the Hales' and found his own treasure—Emma Hale.

Over the next year, it is likely that Joseph worked part-time for both Stowell and Joseph Knight Sr., a man whose conversion would greatly affect the early Church in that region. During this time, Joseph returned to Manchester for his annual meeting with Moroni, and still found time to court Emma and ask for her hand in marriage. Knight, sympathetic toward the young man's cause, later stated, "[Joseph] worked for me until the time that he was married, which I think was February [it was actually January]. . . . I paid him the money and I furnished him with a horse and cutter to go and see his girl down to Mr. Hales's."[10] However, Emma's father did not favor this marriage, and according to Joseph,

On the 18th of January, 1827, we were married, while I was yet employed in the service of Mr. Stoal [Stowell]. Owing to my continuing to assert that I had seen a vision, persecution still followed me, and my wife's father's family were very much opposed to our being married. I was, therefore, under the necessity of taking her elsewhere; so we went and were married at the house of Squire Tarbill, in South Bainbridge, Chenango county, New York. Immediately after my marriage, I left Mr. Stoal's and went to my father's, and farmed with him that season.[11]

The young couple returned to Harmony in August of 1827 for a brief visit. Isaac Hale offered to assist them in settling down near him; he also offered to help Joseph find work.[12] However, the young couple did not move to Harmony until December of that same year, when persecution "became so intolerable that [Joseph] was under the necessity of leaving Manchester."[13]

When they returned to Susquehanna, Joseph and Emma stayed with her parents, keeping the plates in the house, enclosed in a box. When Isaac Hale asked to see them and was refused, he said, "I became dissatisfied, and informed [Joseph] that if there was anything in my house of that description, which I could not be allowed to see, he must take it away; if he did not, I was determined to see it."[14] Shortly thereafter, Joseph and Emma moved into another house on the Hale property, which had been owned by Emma's oldest brother, Jesse.

The winter of 1827-28 was a quiet reprieve from the persecutions. Emma was pregnant and Joseph needed time to care for her and provide for the family. Joseph had time to study the plates, copy some of the characters, and translate them using the Urim and Thummim.

In February of 1828, Martin Harris, a respected farmer and Joseph's friend from Palmyra, came to Harmony by previous arrangement. Joseph gave Martin a transcript that included written characters from the plates as well as their translation. Martin took this manuscript to some scholars in the east, and the positive response he received solidified his confidence in Joseph. Upon his return to Palmyra, Martin arranged his affairs so he could assist Joseph with the translation. He arrived back in Harmony on April 12.

In addition to using the Urim and Thummim in the translation, Joseph also used a seer stone to translate the record. Of one occasion, Martin reported:

> After continued translation, we would become weary, and would go down to the river and exercise by throwing stones out on the river, etc. While so doing on one occasion, I found a stone very much resembling the one used for translating, and on resuming our labor of translation, I put in place the stone that I had found. . . . The Prophet remained silent, unusually and intently gazing in darkness. . . . Much sur-

prised, Joseph exclaimed, "Martin! What is the matter? All is as dark as Egypt!"[15]

Martin went on to say, "My countenance betrayed me,"[16] indicating perhaps that he had tried, but was unable, to secure yet another piece of evidence authenticating Joseph's prophetic work.

The work continued, and by 14 June 1828, they had 116 pages written on foolscap paper (13" X 16"). Martin knew that his wife, Lucy, felt Joseph was try-

ing to defraud the Harrises, and hoping to allay her fears, he asked to take the 116 pages of manuscript to Palmyra to show her. Through the Urim and Thummim, Joseph inquired of the Lord. Twice the request was denied, but Martin persisted in asking and finally he was given permission by the Lord to show them only to certain, specified people. Martin made a covenant to follow these directions, then left for Palmyra.[17]

The day following Martin's departure, Emma gave birth to her first child, a son, who died that same day. She became deathly ill, and for two weeks Joseph cared for her, receiving little rest himself. When she started to recover, Joseph's thoughts turned to Martin's long absence. Knowing his concerns, Emma suggested her mother could care for her while Joseph went to Palmyra to inquire about Martin.[18]

Exhausted physically and emotionally, Joseph traveled to Manchester, and by the end of the trip he was so weak that he required the assistance of a stranger to complete the last four miles to his parents' house. Otherwise, he stated, "he would fall asleep as he was walking along."[19]

Joseph took a little food for nourishment, then sent for Martin Harris. Four tense hours later Martin was seen, "walking with a slow and measured tread towards the house. . . . On coming to the gate, he stopped, instead of passing through, and got upon the fence, and sat there some time with his hat drawn over his eyes." At length, he entered the house.

He was offered some food, so he took a seat at the table and picked up a knife and fork. Then dropping the utensils, he gave an anguished cry. "Oh, I have lost my soul! I have lost my soul!"

LUCY HARRIS

In the summer of 1829, Lucy Harris, frustrated with her husband's continued interest in the translation of the gold plates, entered a complaint against Joseph Smith before a magistrate at the courthouse in Lyons, accusing Joseph of trying to "defraud her husband out of all his property."[1] Martin adamantly defended the Prophet and stated, "I have never seen, in Joseph Smith, a disposition to take any man's money, without giving him a reasonable compensation for the same in return. And as to the plates which he professes to have, gentlemen, if you do not believe it, but continue to resist the truth, it will one day be the means of damning your souls."

It is interesting to note that two years later, W. W. Phelps was imprisoned in this same building. While the complaint lodged against him was for "indebtedness," his debtors let him know the actual reason for his imprisonment was to keep him "from joining the Mormons."[2] In April of 1830, he purchased his own copy of the Book of Mormon and soon became convinced of its truthfulness; the book "filled [him] with hope; . . . with light; . . . with joy, and . . . with satisfaction," he said. "By that book I learned the right way of God."[3]

After Phelps was released from prison, he promptly prepared his family and left Canandaigua for Kirtland, Ohio.

1. Lucy Smith, Biographical Sketches, 134.
2. Bruce A. Van Orden, "By That Book I Learned the Right Way to God": The Conversion of William W. Phelps," in Regional Studies in Latter-day Saint Church History/ New York. Eds. Larry C. Porter, Milton V. Backman Jr. and Susan Easton Black (Provo, Utah: Dept. of Church History and Doctrine, Brigham Young University, 1992), 211.
3. Ibid.

No doubt fearing the worst, Joseph asked him point-blank, "Martin, have you lost that manuscript? Have you broken your oath, and brought down condemnation upon my head, as well as your own?" At Martin's affirmative response, Joseph cried out, "Oh, my God! . . . All is lost! All is lost! What shall I do?"[20]

Joseph learned that not only had Martin lost the 116 pages, but he had also broken his covenant and allowed many people to see the transcript, contrary to his instructions.[21]

Written words would not likely approximate the anguish of soul that Joseph felt at this time, and he remained inconsolable. The first pages of the Book of Mormon would no longer be available to the world. Joseph paced back and forth in the house the entire day until sunset, when he was finally convinced to eat something. Lucy Mack Smith described the feeling that day as though, "the heavens seemed clothed with blackness, and the earth shrouded with gloom."[22]

Martin lost his privilege as scribe, and according to Lucy Smith, was temporally afflicted as "a heavy fog swept over Mr. Harris's fields and blighted all his wheat, so that he lost about two-thirds of his crop, while the fields on the opposite side of the road remained untouched."[23]

The next day Joseph left for Harmony. "We parted with heavy hearts," said Lucy, "for it now appeared that all which we had so fondly anticipated, and which had been the source of so much secret gratification, had in a moment fled, and fled forever."[24] The lost pages, the "Book of Lehi," were no longer available, as the Lord would not allow them to be translated again.[25]

JOSEPH KNIGHT

With their time thus devoted to the translation, Joseph's household was in need of temporal assistance. Many times the needed goods were brought from Colesville by Joseph's former employer, Joseph Knight Sr., who recalled, "I bought a barrel of mackerel and some lined paper for writing. And when I [came] home I bought some nine or ten bushels of grain and five or six bushels [of] potatoes and a pound of tea, and I went down to see him and they were in want."[1]

Throughout his life, Joseph Smith never forgot the compassion of Mr. Knight who "very kindly and considerately brought us a quantity of provisions, in order that we might not be interrupted in the work of translation by the want of such necessaries of life. . . ."[2] The Prophet described Joseph Knight as "faithful and true, and even-handed and exemplary, and virtuous and kind. . . . This was a faithful man in Israel; therefore his name shall never be forgotten."[3]

(Photo shows what was Joseph Knight's land.)

1. William G. Hartley, *They Are My Friends: A History of the Joseph Knight Family, 1825-1850* (Provo, Utah: Grandin Book, 1986), 34.
2. Ibid., 34.
3. Joseph Smith, *History of the Church of Jesus Christ of Latter-day Saints*, ed. B. H. Roberts, 7 vols. (Salt Lake City: Deseret Book, 1978), 1:47.

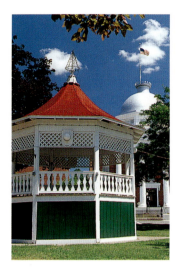

▲ *When Lyons was selected to be the Wayne county seat in 1823, a two-story brick building was raised in the center of the village square to accommodate a jail in the basement and a courthouse on the second floor. This building was the center of all legal activities in Wayne county, which included the town of Palmyra.*

This is the same building where Lucy Harris entered a complaint against Joseph Smith. It is also the building where W. W. Phelps was imprisoned on the false charges of "indebtedness," while in truth, his associates wanted to keep him from joining the Church.

In 1855 a new and larger courthouse was built. The old building was torn down, and a pavilion was established in its place (shown above).

The Urim and Thummim were taken from Joseph for a time, and he was told that they would be returned to him the following September 22.[26] A short time later, the translators were returned briefly for Joseph to receive a revelation. In this heavenly communication, now recorded as Doctrine and Covenants section 3, the young prophet was chastised for his transgressions and for having "feared man more than God" (Doctrine and Covenants 3:7). But he was also given hope, for the Lord said, "Thou art still chosen, and art again called to the work" (Doctrine and Covenants 3:10). This was the first revelation recorded in this dispensation.

As promised, Joseph received the translators in September, and began to translate small sections of the plates as he could on his own. Joseph Knight related that "when Joseph began to translate he was poor . . . and had no one to write for him but his wife, and in the winter, her brother [Reuben] wrote a little for him. . . . "[27] But before the work of translation could be done, Joseph needed to care for temporal concerns and said, "I did not . . . go immediately to translating, but went to laboring with my hands upon a small farm which I had purchased for my family."[28]

Two months later, Joseph Sr. and Lucy traveled to Harmony, concerned that they had not heard from Joseph. There they found their son in good spirits and in possession of the plates and the Urim and Thummim. They stayed with Joseph and Emma for the next three months, which allowed them to become acquainted with Emma's family, who left Joseph's parents with a positive impression.[29]

The year 1829 seems to have been a turning point in Joseph's prophetic life, as his ability to accomplish the work assigned to him and to receive the revelations increased dramatically. When the Prophet's father and his brother Samuel visited him in February, Joseph received a revelation directed to his father. Recorded in Doctrine and Covenants section 4, this revelation, now memorized by missionaries the world over, gives the Christlike characteristics required of those "in the service of God."

A month later, in another revelation, Joseph was told that the Lord would soon "provide the means whereby thou mayest accomplish the thing which I have commanded thee" (Doctrine and Covenants 5:34). It was not long before "means" were provided—for both the translation and for Joseph's temporal affairs.

By divine design, a young school teacher named Oliver Cowdery began boarding with Joseph's parents. After hearing of Joseph's experience, Oliver's heart was moved, and he determined to go to Harmony to learn the truth of the matter for himself. On Sunday, April 5, Oliver Cowdery arrived in Harmony with the prophet's brother Samuel, and within two days, began acting as scribe to Joseph as the translation proceeded. Over the next three months, the two men translated the plates at a humanly impossible rate, completing about 500 printed pages of the Book of Mormon. During these short months, Joseph also received and wrote down eight more revelations, which would be included in the Doctrine and Covenants (sections 6-13). Years later, Oliver would recall, "These were days never to be forgotten—to sit under the sound of a voice dictated by the inspiration of heaven, awakened the utmost gratitude of this bosom!"[30]

After translating the account of the Savior's visit to the Nephites, Joseph and Oliver understood that

This lake-stone schoolhouse, built around 1848, rests on the original foundation of the school where Oliver Cowdery commenced to teach. The old school was a wood frame building, and was moved and incorporated into the house which is seen in the background.

When he started to teach at this school early in 1829, Oliver boarded with the Smiths and became acquainted with the story of the gold plates. His heart was touched, and he determined to go visit Joseph in Harmony. After a few short months of teaching, Oliver became a scribe for the prophet.

▶ *The monument commemorating the restoration of the Aaronic Priesthood is located just west of the McKune cemetery along Highway 171.*

"Upon you my fellow servants, in the name of Messiah I confer the Priesthood of Aaron, which holds the keys of the ministering of angels, and of the gospel of repentance, and of baptism by immersion for the remission of sins; and this shall never be taken again from the earth, until the sons of Levi do offer again an offering unto the Lord in righteousness" (Doctrine and Covenants 13).

"none had authority . . . to administer in the name of Christ . . . and we only waited for the commandment to be given, 'Arise and be baptized.'"[31] On 15 May 1829, Joseph and Oliver retired to the woods to inquire regarding this topic. While praying, they heard the Savior's voice speak peace to them, followed by the appearance of a glorious being, who stated that he was John the Baptist. Acting under the direction of Peter, James, and John, the heavenly messenger laid his hands upon Joseph's and Oliver's heads and conferred upon them the Aaronic Priesthood.

The ancient prophet instructed them to baptize and ordain each other, telling Joseph that he would be known as "the first Elder of the Church, and he [Oliver Cowdery] the second."[32]

Joseph first baptized Oliver, after which Oliver baptized Joseph. As each came out of the water, the Holy Ghost fell upon them and they were filled with the spirit of prophecy. Joseph then ordained Oliver to the Aaronic Priesthood, and Oliver ordained Joseph. Hereafter they saw an increase in their spiritual understanding, noting that they understood scriptural passages "in a manner which we never could attain to previously, nor ever before had thought of."[33]

Following the visit from John the Baptist, Joseph must have felt a tremendous sense of relief. For the first time in the nine years since the First Vision, someone was by his side, saw what he saw, heard what he heard, and could testify along with him regarding the heavenly visitations. For Oliver, "uncertainly had fled, doubt had sunk, no more to rise, while fiction and deception had fled forever!"[34]

Soon after this, Joseph's brother Samuel visited Harmony. Joseph and Oliver eagerly told him of the recent occurrences. Samuel went into the woods to pray, where he became convinced of the truth of what they were saying. On May 25 he became the third person baptized. He then left for Palmyra, "glorifying and praising God."[35] Hyrum arrived a few days later and was quick to accept what Joseph and Oliver taught. Desiring to know what the Lord would have him do, Hyrum was told, "seek not to declare my word, but first seek to obtain my word, and then shall your tongue be loosed" (Doctrine & Covenants 11:21).

The restoration of the higher, or Melchizedek, Priesthood likely occurred while Joseph and Oliver were returning from a visit to Colesville, shortly after the visitation by John the Baptist. In the wilderness between Colesville and Harmony, along the Susquehanna River, Peter, James, and John appeared and conferred upon Joseph and Oliver the Melchizedek Priesthood, bestowing upon them the keys of the apostleship.[36] The authority to act in God's name was once again on the earth, and now the restoration of the kingdom, of which Daniel spoke, could proceed.

As persecution against Joseph in Pennsylvania intensified, Joseph and Oliver accepted an invitation from Peter Whitmer Sr., of Fayette, New York, to come live at his house in order to finish the translation of the Book of Mormon. Peter's son David was an acquaintance of Oliver's; the two had written letters to each other during Oliver's time in Harmony. Near the end of May, David arrived in Harmony with a wagon in which to carry the Prophet and Oliver back to the Whitmer home, where they stayed until the translation was finished, the copyright secured, and its publication started.

▲ *The mound behind the sign (to the right) is where the foundation of Joseph and Emma's home was in Harmony, Pennsylvania.*

Behind is the monument commemorating the restoration of the Aaronic Priesthood, and to the left in the distance is the McKune cemetery.

When Joseph initially approached the twenty-three-year-old E. B. Grandin of Palmyra about publishing the Book of Mormon, he refused. Joseph then went to the publishers in the larger city of Rochester in search of help, but returned to Egbert B. Grandin and persuaded him to print 5,000 copies of the Book of Mormon, at a cost of $3,000. Grandin's reluctance was overcome only after Martin Harris agreed to sign a mortgage on his farm guaranteeing the payment of the printing. If payment was not made, Martin would be required to auction part of his land.[37]

Martin Harris had prospered financially as a farmer in the days before the Restoration, and had earned the respect of the community. Due to his

involvement with Joseph Smith however, Martin lost the support of his wife, and his reputation diminished among the townspeople. Nevertheless, Martin believed Joseph was telling the truth. Perhaps that is one of the reasons why the Lord allowed him to become one of three special witnesses. Only those who have been willing to sacrifice their family, their land, their finances, and their reputation for a righteous cause can approach an understanding of Martin Harris's involvement in the publication of the Book of Mormon. Although some prompting from the Lord was required,[38] Martin did sign the mortgage and later sold part of his farm for $3,000 to make the payment for the book.[39]

After the translation of the plates was completed, Oliver Cowdery made a copy of the manuscript,[40] and in August 1829 the first twenty-four handwritten pages were delivered to Grandin's printing establishment on "Exchange Row." The printing office was on the third floor, the book bindery on the second, and the "Palmyra Bookstore" on the ground level.[41] Written "on folscap [sic] paper" (13 x 16 1/2-inch paper), the manuscript was brought daily by Hyrum, "under his vest, and vest and coat closely buttoned over it. At night [Hyrum] Smith came and got the manuscript and with the same precaution carried it away."[42]

Two major setbacks occurred during the printing of the book. At one point an ex-justice of the peace, Esquire Abner Cole, using the pseudonym Obediah Dogberry, ran a series of articles containing actual excerpts of the Book of Mormon in his newspaper, the *Reflector,* published at the "Bower on Wintergreen Hill."[43] Cole, who also printed his paper at Grandin's press, continued this process

(Opposite page) Typeset trays in Grandin Building. Oliver Cowdery tried his hand at typesetting the first 10-12 pages of the first edition of the Book of Mormon, but turned it all over to John H. Gilbert, the typesetter of the shop. There were approximately 2,000 changes to the original edition due to spelling errors, etc. Apparently, Gilbert had a difficult time reading Oliver's handwriting. However, Gilbert was at a disadvantage because he didn't know anything about the Mormons. For example, he had put in "Gadianton noblers" instead of "Gadianton robbers." John Gilbert also added all the punctuation to the manuscript. He described the pages: "Every chapter, if I remember correctly, was one solid paragraph, without a punctuation mark, from beginning to end."[44] Gilbert himself, with permission from Hyrum, applied the punctuation to the original published Book of Mormon.[45]

◀ *The E.B. Grandin Building printing establishment was located on "Exchange Row" in Palmyra. The printing office was on the third floor, the bindery on the second, with the Palmyra Bookstore on ground level.*

until Joseph traveled from Susquehanna and threatened Cole with legal action.[46]

Next, the townspeople of Palmyra resolved to boycott the book and informed Grandin of their decision. The publisher then put the book on hold until he was once again reassured that the payment would be secure.[47] The book apparently did not sell very well locally, and while traveling with Joseph Smith in the spring of 1830, Joseph Knight Sr. (later a convert to the Church), came upon a panicked Martin Harris, who carried a stack of the books in his arms, proclaiming, "The books will not sell for nobody wants them."[48] He could not have comprehended that the Book of Mormon would "whisper out of the dust" (Isaiah 29:4) to the honest in heart, and during the next 170 years, over 100 million copies of it would be printed and distributed.[49]

Modern-day Susquehanna Valley contains a few historical markers that remind us of these significant early events, the most prominent of which is the monument on the south side of Highway 171, about seven miles east of Interstate 89, commemorating the restoration of the Aaronic Priesthood. West of the monument is a small rise where stones have been placed to show the location of Joseph's and Emma's home. According to Mrs. Helen Hawes, who once lived in the house, the home caught fire from a spark blown by a train "puffing up the heavy grade."[50] A wooden fence surrounds what is left of the foundation of Isaac Hale's home, approximately 150 yards west of the monument, on the opposite side of the road. The well-kept McKune Cemetery, 100 yards east of the monument, contains the tombstone of Joseph and Emma's first child, as well as the headstones of Isaac and Elizabeth Hale.

◄ *This is the type of press that was used in the printing of the Book of Mormon. Ink that was splattered on the walls from the days of actual printing can still be seen on the third floor of the building.*

▼ *Gravesite of Joseph and Emma's infant son who died June 15, 1828, just hours after his birth. This was a time of great sorrow and hardship for the young couple. Not only had they lost their firstborn baby, but Emma had fallen gravely ill. Joseph tenderly and anxiously cared for her day and night, while also quietly agonizing over Martin Harris's failure to return with the 116-page manuscript.*

► (This page and Opposite page) The Palmyra Bookstore was located on the ground floor of the Grandin Building in Palmyra, New York. On March 26, 1830, the Wayne Sentinel published the title page of the Book of Mormon and announced, "The above work, containing about 600 pages, large Duodecimo, is now for sale, wholesale and retail, at the Palmyra Bookstore, By E. B. Grandin."[51]

❧

► (Opposite page) Modern-day crops on the Martin Harris farm. Martin Harris was a prosperous farmer who sacrificed his farm for the printing of the Book of Mormon. Although he would never again be as prosperous in a worldly sense, the harvest he reaped for staying true to his testimony of the Book of Mormon would be more valuable than the richest farmland on earth.

The Susquehanna River, which flows gently on the south side of these sites, has changed little since the early 1800s, a quiet witness to the events of the Restoration that occurred here in the Great Bend.

"Now what do we hear in the gospel we have received? . . . glad tidings from Cumorah! . . . And . . . the voice of God in the chamber of old Father Whitmer, in Fayette, Seneca County . . ."

D & C 128:19-21

Open Bible inside the Peter Whitmer Cabin.

CHAPTER SEVEN

The Whole Church of Christ in a Little Old Log House

Between the Seneca and Cayuga Lakes, prior to the 1800s an "unbroken forest stretched northward . . . to the shores of Lake Ontario," the elevated plateau full of oak trees and maples "rich with the juices of spring's rising sap."[1] Large, red cedars grew on the crags above the lakes, while white pines and hemlock trees made their stands along the streams.[2]

However, by the time Peter Whitmer Sr. moved his family to the Fayette area around 1810, this fairly level region was already becoming a "very productive" agricultural community, created largely by the Pennsylvanian Germans who had initially settled there.[3] For many settlers, including the Whitmers, this place was simply a temporary home; as the frontier of America expanded, a great number would continue westward.

Peter Whitmer and his wife, Mary Musselman Whitmer, had left their home in Harrisburg, Pennsylvania, to move to New York. David, their fourth child, was nearly four at the time, having been born 7 January 1805.

Peter Whitmer agreed to purchase a one-hundred-acre parcel of land located almost halfway between the northern points of the two largest Finger Lakes, Cayuga and Seneca, in the township of Fayette, Seneca County, just a few miles south of Waterloo.[4] Over the years, three more children were born to the Whitmers, bringing the total to eight, and as the family grew they became quite respected in the community. The family attended the Zion's Church, which had been created jointly by members of the German Reformed and Lutheran denominations.[5]

On a business trip to Palmyra in 1828, David Whitmer heard the townspeople talking of one Joseph Smith and some golden plates. On this same trip, David became acquainted with Oliver Cowdery, who was boarding with the Smiths and who told David he was convinced there was something to the story. Thereafter, Oliver kept David informed through a regular correspondence. Around 1 April 1829, Oliver Cowdery and Samuel Smith arrived at the Whitmer cabin while enroute to Harmony, Pennsylvania, where Joseph was living. Oliver informed David that as soon as he had any information regarding the truth about the plates, he would send word back to David and his family.[6] Not long afterward, David received the promised letters, and with them, Oliver's conviction that the work was divine. David shared these letters with his family, no doubt creating some excitement and preparing them for a letter in which Oliver discussed the possibility that he and Joseph might come to the Whitmer home for a time. Peter Whitmer Sr. gave permission for them to stay at his house for as long as they needed in order to finish the translation, and David volunteered to provide their transportation to Fayette.[7]

David had received Oliver's letter toward the end of May, which was planting season in western New York, and he felt he needed to plow over the wheat and sow plaster on his fields before he could leave for Harmony. To his surprise, David found that he was able to plow in one day what would have normally taken two. He was even more amazed the following day when he went to get the plaster that was stored by his sister's house. Finding it gone, he inquired of his sister, who told him that on the previous day her children had begged her to watch some "men sow plaster in the field, saying they never saw anybody sow plaster so fast in their lives." When David's sister went to the field, she "saw three

(Opposite page) The Peter Whitmer Cabin in Fayette, NY. In 1844 at a conference held in Nauvoo, Sidney Rigdon reminisced about his visit to the Whitmer home after his conversion: "I met the whole church of Christ in a little old log house about 20 feet square, near Waterloo, N.Y. and we began to talk about the kingdom of God as if we had the world at our command; we talked with great confidence, and talked big things. Although we were not many people, we had big feelings. We knew . . . that the Church would become as large as it is today . . . We talked about the people coming as doves to the windows; and that nations should flock unto it."[8]

Seneca Lake, NY. Joseph noted, "We found the people of Seneca county . . . friendly, and disposed to enquire into the truth . . . From this time forth many became believers, and some were baptized."[9] Among those baptized in June 1829 in Seneca Lake, a beautiful and transparent sheet of water in Western New York, were Hyrum Smith, David Whitmer, and Peter Whitmer Jr. In September 1830, Parley P. Pratt was also baptized here by Oliver Cowdery.

men at work in the field, as the children said, but, supposing that [David] had hired some help . . . gave the subject no further attention."[10] Interpreting this as a divine sign, David immediately left for Pennsylvania, arriving there two days later.

When David, Oliver, and Joseph arrived back in Fayette around June 1, they were greeted, not only by the entire Whitmer family anxiously awaiting news of the work, but an entire community that was more open to what was being revealed than any other they had previously encountered.

The translation resumed immediately upon their arrival in Fayette, in a hot upstairs room of the Whitmer cabin. But Oliver was no longer the sole

scribe. Three others began to assist him—John Whitmer primarily,[11] but also Christian Whitmer and Emma Smith.[12] The three Whitmer boys still living at home, David, John, and Peter Jr., were particularly enthusiastic about the work, and each received a personal revelation from the Lord regarding their duties.[13] All was going very well, and the work continued forward unhindered, "from morning till night."[14] But with all the attention focused on the work of translation, Peter's wife, Mary, felt the overwhelming burden of an increasing amount of household and farm chores.

One day, as she went to milk the cows in the barn, Mary was met by an elderly man. "You have been very faithful and diligent in your labors," he said to her, "but you are tired because of the increase of your toil, it is proper therefore that you should receive a witness that your faith may be strengthened."[15] He then showed her the gold plates, which were hidden in the barn. The elderly man was likely Moroni.

After the loss of the initial 116 pages of manuscript by Martin Harris, Joseph and Oliver commenced translating, starting with the book of Mosiah, and proceeded until they finished the book of Moroni. Only then did they return to the start of the Nephite record and translate the small plates, which cover the books of Nephi through the Words of Mormon.[16] Nearing the end of the translation of Nephi's words, they once again came upon the concept of the need for witnesses for the Book of Mormon.[17] When the book was finished in late June of 1829, or very near the end of its completion, Joseph sent word to his parents, who prepared immediately to depart for Fayette, bringing with them an elated Martin Harris.[18] Arriving at the

▲ *This beautiful building on the Whitmer farm serves as both a chapel and a visitors' center. It was not far from this location where the three witnesses were shown the gold plates by Moroni. "We accordingly made choice of a piece of woods convenient to Mr. Whitmer's house, to which we retired, and having knelt down, we began to pray in much faith to Almighty God . . . when presently . . . an angel stood before us."*[19]

◀ *Hathaway Creek (Crooked Creek) on the Smith farm. Baptisms were performed a little downstream at the Stoddard mill site. "We repaired from the meeting (at the Smith log cabin) to the water's edge, and, at [Joseph's] request, I baptized several persons."*[20] *Parley P. Pratt.*

Whitmer cabin, Martin, along with David Whitmer and Oliver Cowdery, felt impressed to ask Joseph if they would be the three witnesses. In a revelation responding to this, the Lord stated unto the three: "You shall have a view of the plates, and also of the breastplate, the sword of Laban, the Urim and Thummim. . . . And it is by your faith that you shall obtain a view of them, even by that faith which was had by the prophets of old" (Doctrine and Covenants 17:1-2).

One morning, after devotional services, Joseph approached Martin and said, "Martin Harris, you have got to humble yourself before your God this day, that you may obtain a forgiveness of your sins. If you do, it is the will of God that you should look upon the plates, in company with Oliver Cowdery and David Whitmer."[21] Within minutes, Martin joined Joseph and Oliver, and retrieved David from the field where he was plowing.[22] They then retired to a "piece of woods convenient to Mr. Whitmer's house . . . and having knelt down, we began to pray in much faith."[23] Each in turn offered a prayer, and the sequence was repeated, but the manifestation did not come. Martin, feeling that he was the limiting factor, withdrew himself from the group, and the remaining three continued to pray.

Within minutes of Martin's departure, a light appeared, and Moroni stood before them with the plates in his hands, which he showed to the kneeling men.[24] David then records that "a table was set before us and on it the records were placed . . . [as well as] the breast plates, the Ball of Directors, the Sword of Laban and other plates."[25] David, having his first angelic visitation, was addressed directly by Moroni: "David, Blessed is the Lord, and he that

keeps His commandments."[26] The three heard a voice, "from out of the bright light above us, saying, 'These plates have been revealed by the power of God, and they have been translated by the power of God. The translation of them which you have seen is correct, and I command you to bear record of what you now see and hear.'"[27]

Joseph, leaving David and Oliver, found Martin alone in fervent prayer. He joined with him, and within a short time this same vision was repeated. With this, Martin cried out, "'Tis enough; 'tis enough; mine eyes have beheld; mine eyes have beheld," then jumping to his feet, Martin rejoiced, shouting "Hosanna" and commenced praising God.[28]

▲ *Many long, hot hours of work in finishing the translation of the Book of Mormon occurred in the upper chamber of the Whitmer cabin—small quarters became a place of revelation.*

◄ *(Opposite page) After Moroni appeared to the Three Witnesses, Joseph was overjoyed to no longer be the only person to have seen the gold plates. This is the very bed onto which Joseph threw himself to share this happy news with his parents.*

No longer was Joseph alone in trying to convince the world that he had the plates. Arriving back at the cabin, he threw himself onto the bed in the room where his father and mother were, and exclaimed:

> Father, mother, you do not know how happy I am; the Lord has now caused the plates to be shown to three more besides myself. They have seen an angel, who has testified to them, and they will have to bear witness to the truth of what I have said . . . and I feel as if I was relieved of a burden which was almost too heavy for me to bear, and it rejoices my soul, that I am not any longer to be entirely alone in the world.[29]

Each copy of the Book of Mormon, from the first 5,000 copies to the millions that have followed, contains the testimony of the three witnesses—David Whitmer, Oliver Cowdery, and Martin Harris—testifying to the world of the book's divine origins.

The next day, Joseph Sr. and Lucy returned home to their small log cabin, followed a few days later by Joseph Jr., Oliver, and several members of the Whitmer family, coming to arrange for the printing of the book. There, in the Smith home, eight men were privileged to see and handle the plates, under Joseph's direction. They, too, would testify to the world that they had seen and touched the plates.

After returning to Fayette, Joseph and Oliver were both anxious to receive the blessing mentioned by John the Baptist in Susquehanna, of being ordained as elders in the Melchizedek Priesthood (having already received this priesthood

◀ (Opposite page) Downstairs in the Whitmer Cabin. Thomas B. Marsh, Parley P. Pratt, and Orson Pratt were among those who heard the gospel preached in this small cabin.

❧

◀ Kitchen and hearth in the Whitmer Cabin. Fifty to sixty people gathered here on April 6, 1830, to see the official organization of The Church of Jesus Christ of Latter-day Saints. On June 9, 1830, the first conference of the restored Church was also held at the Whitmer farm. The Spirit was abundant, and "many of our number prophesied, whilst others had the heavens opened to their view, and were so overcome that we had to lay them on beds or other convenient places." These manifestations were given for the purpose of inspiring "our hearts with joy unspeakable, and fill us with awe and reverence for that Almighty Being, by whose grace we had been called to [this work]. . . . Still more were baptized into the Church that day."[30]

Inside the visitors' center at the Whitmer farm. The statue of Peter, James, and John bestowing the Melchizedek Priesthood, and the stained glass windows representing the First Vision and Joseph acquiring the gold plates, depict some of the most significant events in the restoration of the gospel.

from Peter, James, and John), and so made this a subject of solemn prayer. One day, while seeking the Lord's guidance in the chamber of the Whitmers' cabin, the two heard the Lord's voice commanding them that they should ordain each other as elders in the "Church of Jesus Christ."[31] This was not to be done, however, until some believers were assembled and could sanction those ordinations with a vote. As given by revelation, now known as Doctrine and Covenants 20, the

date for this meeting would be 6 April 1830, and the announcement of this date was spread by word of mouth.

On that date, in the 20-by-30-foot Whitmer cabin, approximately sixty people gathered for the official organization of "The Church of Jesus Christ,"[32] with approximately twenty of them coming from Colesville, at least a hundred miles away.[33] Aside from Joseph, five men in the group were designated as part of the official chartered organization, in accordance with New York statutes.

The meeting was simple. Opening with solemn prayer, Joseph called for a vote to know whether those present accepted him and Oliver as teachers and spiritual leaders in the Church; the vote was affirmative. Joseph then laid his hands on Oliver and ordained him an elder in the Church of Jesus Christ, and Oliver ordained Joseph. The sacrament was blessed and given to those present, then Joseph and Oliver laid their hands upon each "individual member of the church,"[34] and through the power of the Melchizedek Priesthood, officially confirmed them members of the Church and bestowed upon them the gift of the Holy Ghost. Others were called out from the assembled group and ordained to various offices in the priesthood as directed by the Spirit. A revelation naming Joseph as "a seer, a translator, a prophet, an apostle of Jesus Christ" was received in the presence of all (Doctrine and Covenants 21:1).

Though simple, the meeting was profound, and the Holy Ghost was poured out on those present. Some prophesied, and all were moved to "rejoice exceedingly."[35] A few, who had come into the meeting unsure of their convictions, left convinced of the truth and were accepted into the Church by joining others who elected to be baptized that day, possibly in a nearby creek or in the great Seneca Lake. Those baptized included the Prophet's parents, Martin Harris, and Orrin Porter Rockwell, a friend of Joseph's. Even Joseph was overwhelmed emotionally when his own father, who to that time had refused to join with any other sect, was baptized. Joseph Knight recorded, "When Mr. Smith came out of the water, Joseph stood upon the shore, and taking his father by the hand, he exclaimed, with tears of joy, 'Oh, my God! Have I lived to see my own father baptized into the true Church of Jesus Christ!'"[36]

The Whitmer cabin continued, from that time until the departure of the saints, to be a place of gathering, instruction, edification, and acceptance into the Church of Jesus Christ.

With the publication of the Book of Mormon and the organization of the Church, Joseph was called to do yet another work, "a great work . . . [to be done] that he may do the work of translation for the salvation of souls."[37] The translation was that of the King James version of the Bible. On October 8 of the previous year, Joseph and Oliver had purchased a large pulpit-style Bible from Grandin's bookstore for $3.75, and by June of 1830 they were making notations in the book, giving further enlightenment on the ancient text. The first handwritten entry was given as a revelation to Joseph regarding "the words of God, which he spake unto Moses at a time when Moses was caught up into an exceedingly high mountain," now the first chapter in the modern Pearl of Great Price (Moses 1:1).

▶ *A dam existed near this site on Hathaway Creek where Russell Stoddard's mill once stood. Many believers were baptized here.*

 Kendig Creek, which runs near the Whitmer farm, is reported to be one of the sites used for baptism in the early days of the Church. On the day the church was organized, Joseph Smith was overwhelmed when his father was baptized. "Oh, my God! have I lived to see my own father baptized into the true Church of Jesus Christ!"[38]

The translation proceeded with the Book of Genesis, which was completed by April of 1831, at which time the Lord directed Joseph to translate the New Testament.[39] Assisted by Oliver Cowdery, John Whitmer, Emma, and eventually Sidney Rigdon, Joseph completed the New Testament by 2 February 1833, and once again directed his attention to the Old Testament. Now many "plain and precious things" (1 Nephi 13:28) had been restored for the purpose of the "salvation of mine own elect" (Doctrine & Covenants 35:20).

To escape the persecution in Pennsylvania, Joseph and Emma moved from Harmony to Fayette in September where the second conference of the Church lasted for three days, September 26-28, and sixty-two members were accounted for. At this conference, and in subsequent revelations, four men were called to go on a mission "unto the Lamanites" (Doctrine and Covenants 28:8).[40] On October 18 these men—Oliver Cowdery, Peter Whitmer Jr., Ziba Peterson, and Parley P. Pratt—started a 1500-mile westward expedition, a journey that had a tremendous impact on the young church.

From there, the missionaries headed west towards Independence, Missouri, once again preparing the way for the members of the Church who would come later.

No minutes were taken for the third conference of the Church, held January 2 of the following year at the Whitmer home, but a commandment was given instructing the Saints in New York to relocate to the area of Kirtland, Ohio.[41] This revelation was greeted by some of the saints in Fayette with mixed emotions, but the truly converted proceeded to leave lands, farms, jobs, and all that they had worked for, to follow a living prophet and the restored Church of Jesus Christ into an unfamiliar land.

Joseph, in the company of Emma and a few others, left Fayette in January 1831 in a sleigh destined for Kirtland, Ohio. By April 1, Peter Whitmer Sr. had sold his farm,[42] and by May 3 or 4, the saints in Seneca county had started their long trip west on the freshly opened canals.[43]

The Whitmers left behind a small cabin, seated on a plateau between the lakes, where an ancient record had been translated and witnesses called to examine the record, a place where a church had begun and twenty revelations, revered as scripture, had been given. Said Orson Pratt of the Whitmer home, "That house will, no doubt, be celebrated for ages to come as the one chosen by the Lord in which to make known the first elements of the organization of His Kingdom in the latter days."[44]

Around 1950, William L. Powell, a Latter-day Saint tenant on the Whitmer farm, discovered the rock foundation of the original Whitmer cabin while he was working on the farm. The foundation was laid with "very small rocks most of them and they were layed in a trench about a foot wide. Just about the width of a log."[45] By 1980 the cabin had been rebuilt, and on April 6 of that year, President Spencer W. Kimball, twelfth President of the Church, dedicated the structure and presided from it by satellite over part of the April general conference of the Church. In 1830, only fifty or sixty people had been able to hear a prophet speak; now millions could share this privilege.

▲Whitmer farmland. The crops grown here were generously shared, providing physical nourishment for many saints. Here, also, the seeds were planted for the growth of the young Church which would nourish the souls of saints worldwide.

CHAPTER EIGHT

Colesville and South Bainbridge

The valley "so fertile and so thoroughly culti-vated that the beauty of the val-ley when viewed from an adjacent hill is often the theme for the poet's lyre."

Overlooking the Susquehanna valley just south of Colesville.

In the valley of the upper Susquehanna, the river "is a broad and majestic stream, with a moderate current, the water pure and sparkling at most seasons of the year; but the water is usually shallow and flows over a diluvial bed, which, when the water is low, gives it for miles the handsomest ripple imaginable."[1] Heading in a southwest direction through most of the valley, the river then bends to a more southerly course at the town of Colesville, on its way to the Great Bend in Pennsylvania. The valley, "so fertile and so thoroughly cultivated that the beauty of the valley when viewed from an adjacent hill is often the theme for the poet's lyre,"[2] is created of sandy loam and alluvium, ascending gradually up the "high and handsomely rounded"[3] hills 300 to 500 feet above the river.

Two counties adjoin here where Joseph Smith worked for most of the year 1826, and where a number of people came to believe on his experience. To the west and south, extending down to the Pennsylvania border, is Broome County. The earliest permanent settlement of the region, the township of Colesville was begun in 1785.

To the east lay Chenango County and the township of Clinton, originally named after the governor of the state; the township was later renamed Jericho, and then Bainbridge. Over time, two distinct centers of population developed in the township, and the people of "South Bainbridge" became disgruntled with the inconvenience of traveling to "North Bainbridge" in order to perform legal affairs. Eventually they pursued, and achieved, the creation of their own township,[4] and in the spirit of one-upmanship, changed the village name from South Bainbridge to Afton, after a small river in England, because the letter A came before B.[5]

◄ (Opposite page) Pickerel Pond is located on the property that was once owned by Joseph Knight, Sr. in Colesville, and is reported to be the site of some of the Colesville baptisms. The Knights were the first family, aside from the Smiths, to accept Joseph Smith's story, and they became the core of what would become the Colesville Branch. After their conversion, the Knight family were persecuted by many of their neighbors. "That night our wagons were turned over and wood piled on them, and some sunk in the water, rails were piled against our doors, and chains sunk in the stream and a great deal of mischief done."[6]

◄ The Susquehanna River between Colesville and Harmony. Early pioneers in this region, mostly from New England and from northern Pennsylvania, were not wealthy and were forced to live off the land as best as they could. Many made their living by lumbering, transporting the wood down the river. When the water was high, "fleets of rafts, flat boats and arks were numerous upon the swift tides and the scene was a picturesque and animated one."[7]

99

Captain Joseph Peck, famous as a Vermont sufferer, moved to Bainbridge around 1789, but his daughter, Polly, stayed behind in Vermont in order to marry Joseph Knight. Some twenty years later, Joseph and Polly Knight followed her father to the Bainbridge region, and then eventually downstream to Colesville.[8]

Another early Bainbridge pioneer was Josiah Stowell. He was described as "a man of much force of character, of indomitable will, and well fitted as a pioneer in the unbroken wilderness. . . . He had been educated in the spirit of orthodox puritanism. . . . He was a very industrious [and] exemplary man."[9] Josiah married Miriam Bridgeman, the daughter of Orlando Bridgeman, who had originally settled in the area between Vermont and New York, which had come under dispute. Orlando was one of the "Vermont Sufferers" to receive land in Bainbridge when the land claimed by both states was given to Vermont.[10]

By 1825, Josiah had acquired over eight hundred acres of land[11] and had built mills on his property that "excited the envy of many of his less fortunate neighbors."[12] In October 1825, Josiah sent for, and hired, Joseph Smith who convinced the old gentleman to desist in his efforts to find a lost Spanish silver mine. Nevertheless, Josiah retained Joseph's services, seeing that his strength and skills could be used to the benefit of Josiah's extensive holdings. After a short return to Manchester in late 1825, Joseph went to South Bainbridge to work on Josiah Stowell's land, remaining in the region for most of the next year.

While thus employed in Bainbridge, Joseph became acquainted with Joseph Knight, who lived in Colesville, three miles downriver from Josiah Stowell's land. Although not as prosperous as the older Stowell,

Joseph Knight had accumulated sufficient property that he needed to hire extra seasonal help to work on the land, in his grist mill, and with his two carding machines.[13] Knight, a Universalist, raised his children "in a genteel and respectable manner" and was himself "a sober, honest man, generally respected and beloved by his neighbors and acquaintances."[14] In 1826, according to his son, Newel Knight, the senior Knight "employed . . . a young man by the name of Joseph Smith, Jun., to whom I was particularly attached. His noble deportment, his faithfulness, his kind address, could not fail to win the esteem of those who had the pleasure of his acquaintance."[15]

 (Opposite page) The valley of the Susquehanna between Colesville and Afton (South Bainbridge). Some of the land on the far side of the valley belonged to Josiah Stowell. Today, little seems to have changed in this area. Farming is still the main economy, and some of the houses from the early 1800s, such as the Joseph Knight home across the river from Ninevah, have been remodeled but are still in use.

VERMONT SUFFERERS

In the early days of this country, some settlers had the misfortune of laying claim to a section of land between Vermont and New York. Because of the ambiguity in the charters given by King Charles II of England to the various colonies, both Vermont and New York felt entitled to a section of land between them. They refused the jurisdiction of the state of Vermont, but the "Yorkers" received little support from their mother state.

Most of them settled around the town of Guilford, where they attempted to live peaceably, but were harassed by Ethan Allen and his famous Green Mountain Boys, who burned homes, took possessions, and whipped the "Yorkers." Tensions subsided briefly during the Revolutionary War, only to resurface at the war's end. Feelings ran high, although only two people died in the conflict that spanned fourteen years.

In 1784 the "Yorkers" lost their rights, and their movement was put to an end when an overwhelming 300 Vermonters descended upon Guilford. Given land in south-central New York 200 miles away in compensation for their losses, these people were known as the "Vermont Sufferers," and the eight square miles granted to them was in the township of Bainbridge.[1]

1. Ann Christle Tobey, "The Vermont Sufferers" (master's thesis, Columbia University, 1958), 22.

▲ *The home of Josiah Stowell is still in use and stands along Highway 7, three miles south of Afton village. His farm, where Joseph worked, extends up the graceful hills behind the house and on the north side of the current railroad tracks.*

▶ *(Opposite page) This fireplace mantle once stood in the house of Squire Tarbell, and is now found in the home of Afton town historian, Charles Decker.*

The house of Squire Tarbell, where Joseph and Emma were married, stood for many years at the entrance of the Afton fair grounds and was used as a dining hall and exhibition building; eventually it was sold at a public auction and torn down.[16]

Today, a New York State marker outside the fairgrounds indicates the location of this house where the prophet's marriage occurred.

The Knights befriended young Joseph Smith throughout his periodic employment with them, and a particularly strong relationship developed between Joseph and Newel, as they worked together.[17] Late in November of 1826, Joseph finally shared with the Knights the story of the angel Moroni and the gold plates. Initially, only Father Knight and his son Joseph Jr. believed what they were told, but in time the entire family came to believe their young friend.[18] Their belief in Joseph's words would establish the Knight family as the core of believers who would eventually become the Colesville branch of the restored Church.

During his time in the Bainbridge and Colesville region, Joseph courted Emma Hale, and in January 1827 married her in the house of Squire Tarbill in South Bainbridge.

When the Church of Jesus Christ was officially organized on 6 April 1830 in Fayette, twenty people from the Colesville region, although unknown by name, were in attendance.[19] Soon after this meeting, Joseph Smith traveled to Colesville and commenced to teach the Knights as well as many of their neighbors. During this visit, a most remarkable event occurred. Newel Knight, who attended the meetings regularly, was admonished by Joseph Smith to pray vocally in public, although he avoided the opportunity. One morning Newel went into the woods, "where, according to his own account afterwards, he made several attempts to pray, but could scarcely do so, feeling that he had not done his duty, in refusing to pray in the presence of others. He began to feel uneasy, and continued to feel worse both in mind and body, until, upon reaching his own house, his appearance was such as to alarm his wife very much."

Newel's wife sent for Joseph Smith, who "found him suffering very much in his mind, and his body acted upon in a very strange manner; his visage and limbs distorted and twisted in every shape and appearance possible to imagine; and finally he was caught up off the floor of the apartment, and tossed about most fearfully."[20]

Neighbors and relatives soon gathered about, and with eight or nine neighbors witnessing the scene, Joseph Smith took Newel's hand and commanded the evil spirit, in the name of Jesus Christ, to depart. Newel later related that he saw the devil leave.

This is the first recorded miracle of the restored Church, an event that created believers out of those who witnessed it.

After the first conference of the Church on June 9, Joseph, along with others from the Fayette area, returned to Colesville, where they found many in the area desiring baptism. One Saturday, they built a dam across a creek (possibly the creek on the Knight property, which flowed from Pickerel pond) with the intent of performing the baptisms the following day, but a mob, doing their work in the dark, destroyed the dam that the Saints had built. In spite of the opposition, the believers gathered on Sunday for the purpose of preaching and teaching, which gathering was also attended by those "who had torn down our dam, and who seemed desirous to give us trouble."[21]

Early Monday morning, before the antagonists could be made aware, the dam was repaired. Thirteen persons were baptized, including Joseph Sr. and Polly Knight, Joseph Knight Jr., and Emma. Seeing this, the mob started to regather, so the Saints finished the baptisms and quickly gathered in the Joseph

Knight home. Being heckled there, the small group fled to Newel Knight's home, where it was only with "great prudence on our part, and reliance in our Heavenly Father, that [the mob was] kept from laying violent hands upon us."[22] But before the newly baptized members could be confirmed, a constable arrived with a warrant for the arrest of Joseph Smith and carried him off to South Bainbridge.

The following day, a trial ensued in which Joseph was charged with being a disorderly person. Joseph Knight hired the lawyers to defend the prophet, while Josiah Stowell and two of his daughters testified on behalf of the prophet. But in spite of the frivolous and weak charges, the delay of the trial allowed sufficient time that another warrant from Broome county could be issued for Joseph's arrest.

Once again, at trial the following day in the next county, Joseph's innocence was apparent, and the same two lawyers who had defended him the previous day "spoke like men inspired of God, whilst those who were arrayed against me trembled under the sound of their voices, and quailed before them like criminals before a bar of justice."[23] Years later Joseph's lawyer, Mr. Reid, would say, "Yes, sir, let me say to you that not one blemish nor spot was found against his [Joseph's] character."[24]

After the trials, Joseph escaped the mob and returned to Pennsylvania. The mob also went after the Knights who awoke the day of the second trial to find that their "wagons were turned over and wood piled on them, and some sunk in the water, rails were piled against our doors, and chains sunk in the stream and a great deal of mischief done."[25]

In spite of the threats he faced in Colesville, Joseph was determined to return so that those who

(Opposite page) In the wilderness between Colesville, New York and Harmony, Pennsylvania, Peter, James, and John appeared to Joseph Smith and Oliver Cowdery along the banks of the Susquehanna River and bestowed upon them the higher priesthood.

had been baptized could be confirmed; and so, within days of his having escaped from the mobs there, Joseph returned to Colesville with Oliver. Once again, opposition arose quickly and the two men were required to flee for their safety. After traveling all night, they arrived safely at Harmony.

JOSIAH STOWELL

What became of the sixty-one-year-old Josiah Stowell is of interest. Although some records indicate that he left with the other Saints he did not settle in Ohio, but instead ended up residing in Smithboro, New York, downstream along the Susquehanna River, until his death.[1] There he stayed for over a decade, all the while maintaining a conviction that Joseph Smith, whom he had hired to search for silver at one time, was a prophet of God. In a letter written in 1843 by Martha Campbell at the request of Josiah, he stated that he "never staggered at the foundation of the work, for he knew too much concerning it," and his faith "con-

cerning the work of the Lord" was firm. His great desire was to gather with the Saints in Nauvoo.[2] In another letter written by his son, Josiah Jr., the older man proclaimed his belief in Joseph Smith as "a seer and a prophet."[3] A man who had searched for treasures in the earth, Josiah Stowell found his treasure in the Book of Mormon and in a modern-day prophet.

1. Larry C. Porter, "Organizational Origins of the Church of Jesus Christ, 6 April 1830" in *Regional Studies in Latter-day Saint Church History/ New York.* Eds. Larry C. Porter, Milton V. Backman Jr. and Susan Easton Black (Provo, Utah: Dept. of Church History and Doctrine, Brigham Young University, 1992), 208.

2. 210.

3. *Church News,* May 12, 1985, 10.

During this time of spiritual growth and temporal frustrations, Joseph once again returned to visit the saints of Colesville, along with Hyrum, John Whitmer, and David Whitmer. Having exercised faith through prayer that they could make this trip unmolested, and that the eyes of the molesters would be blinded, the group passed through the midst of some of the most bitter enemies of the Prophet without being recognized. Rejoicing, the Saints met together at last, and those who were baptized two months earlier were finally confirmed.[26]

That fall, others, such as Hyrum Smith and his family, came to Colesville; Orson Pratt also came, while serving his first mission. In all, about sixty persons accepted the message and joined the Church in the Colesville region. Some baptisms were reportedly performed in Joseph Knight's Pickerell Pond. In spite of the severe persecutions that arose in this valley, it was in this place that the first branch of The Church of Jesus Christ of Latter-day Saints was officially organized.[27] Despite future moves to Ohio, and then to Missouri, the members of "the Colesville branch" stayed together, recognized as a group characterized by its unity.

After the revelation in January of 1831, directing the Saints to move to Kirtland, Ohio,[28] the Colesville members traveled to Ithaca, where wagons were replaced by boats that carried them along Cayuga Lake, over the Seneca and Erie Canals, and across Lake Erie to the Kirtland region. Although the township of Colesville still exists, there is no village by that name; instead, the village across the river from where the Knights lived is now known as Nineveh.

In this peaceful valley, on a quiet day, one can almost imagine a wagon train heading out of the valley on its way to Ohio.

"I arose, pulled off my apron, washed my hands and started with him, with my sleeves rolled up to my shoulders, and went a distance of one mile, where he baptized me in a small stream in the woods."

HEBER C. KIMBALL

A remnant of the dam, a few beams, and rocks from the fireplace of Brigham's mill can be seen along the stream where two men were baptized, one to become a prophet, the other an apostle of Jesus Christ.

CHAPTER NINE

Spiritual Manifestations in Mendon

At Boughton Hill Road, which is at the next major crossroads to the south on Mendon-Ionia Road, stands what is left of the Tomlinson Inn, where the gift of tongues was made manifest. The old inn has since been incorporated into a newer house. Solomon Kimball's house stands three-quarters of a mile further up Boughton Hill Road.

At Boughton Hill Road, which is at the next major crossroads to the south on Mendon-Ionia Road, stands what is left of the Tomlinson Inn, where the gift of tongues was made manifest. The old inn has since been incorporated into a newer house. Solomon Kimball's house stands three-quarters of a mile further up Boughton Hill Road.

The three-day trip by stagecoach from Canandaigua to Buffalo cost $2.00. For the wearied traveler on this route, a stop at the inn at the junction of Tomlinson Corners offered a refreshing opportunity to rest, eat in the "grand tavern," dance in the "ballroom," or listen to impromptu speakers talking about the pertinent topics of the day.[1] This busy stagecoach stop was located fifteen miles southwest of Rochester in the township of Mendon, where "the land is good, a part of it rather grass than grain land, with a handsome surface."[2]

At this very inn, in the year 1830, Samuel Smith placed a copy of the newly published Book of Mormon in the hands of Phineas Young, an itinerant Methodist preacher.[3] That book, along with another copy given to Young's brother-in-law John P. Greene,[4] would, over time, be instrumental in the conversion of the entire Young family into the newly restored church, "where they have continued faithful members. . . . And through their faithfulness and zeal, some of them have become as great and honorable men as ever stood upon the earth."[5] It was Phineas' brother, Brigham Young who led the greatest migration of a people in America across the country to settle in the Rocky Mountains.

In 1817, when Brigham Young was sixteen years old, he was instructed by his widowed father, John, "You now have your time; go and provide for yourself."[6] From his home in Aurelius, New York, Brigham went to nearby Auburn, where he apprenticed with John C. Jeffries and became a skilled carpenter, painter, and glazier. In search of other opportunities, he moved to Port Byron in 1823, where he not only found employment, but Miriam Angeline Works as well, whom he wed the following year, and with whom he had a baby daughter, Elizabeth, in 1825. By the end of the year 1828, Brigham Young had moved with his family to Mendon, New York, where his father and many of his siblings were residing.[7] While living with his father, Brigham built a house and a mill on the land that his father owned, "a beautiful sweep of very productive, sandy soil watered by small streams."[8]

The two-story mill that Brigham constructed was unique: its 45-by-20-foot foundation straddled Trout Creek, a stream that ran through the back side

◀ *Interior of Tomlinson Inn.*
The room you can see through
the doorway is where the follow-
ing event took place. "In April
1830 I [Phineas Young] was on
my way home from the town of
Lima, where I had been to
preach. I stopped at the house of
a man by the name of
Tomlinson to get some dinner.
While engaged in a conversation
with the family, a young man
came in, and walking aross the
room to where I was sitting,
held a book toward me, saying,
'There is a book, sir, I wish you
to read.' The thing appeared so
novel to me that for a moment I
hesitated, saying, 'Pray sir,
what book have you?' [He
answered] 'The Book of
Mormon, or, as it is called by
some, the golden bible.'"⁹

The young man was
Samuel Smith, the prophet
Joseph's younger brother.
Phineas Young accepted the
challenge, which led to the con-
version of his entire family,
including his brother, Brigham
Young.

of the John Young property. A dam located four feet upstream from the mill created enough water pressure that when the water was released into the chute running underneath the building, it created sufficient power to run a turning lathe in the shop on the first floor. The fireplace on the first floor also doubled as a forge for blacksmith-type work, and an oven for the making of bricks. Evidence also indicates that Brigham and his family at least temporarily lived on the second floor of the building, where there was "a bed in one corner, a cupboard for dishes in another, a table and a few splint bottom chairs—and a fireplace."[10]

Just as he had in Auburn, Brigham Young developed a reputation in Mendon as an excellent craftsman and woodworker as he glazed windows and built houses and chairs. But his dear friend Heber C. Kimball later described some of the more menial tasks they performed: "when we worked in the hayfield, we would work from sunrise to sunset. . . . We would rake and bind after a cradler for a bushel of wheat a day, and chop wood, with snow to our waist for eighteen cents a cord, and take our pay in corn at seventy-five cents a bushel."[11]

After the birth of another daughter in June 1830, named Vilate after Heber C. Kimball's wife, Brigham and his family left Mendon for a time when his work took him away; they returned in 1832. At some point, Miriam contracted tuberculosis, which impeded her ability to work. Brigham's day thus consisted not only of working in the mill, but also of caring for the family. A local resident later recalled, "There could scarcely be a more kind and affectionate husband and father than [Brigham] was, and few men in his circumstances would have provided better for their families."[12]

Heber C. Kimball was another man who would play a significant role in the restored Church. Born in 1801, the same year as Brigham Young, he moved with his family from Vermont to West Bloomfield, New York, at the age of ten. His father's success as a blacksmith, farmer, and jack-of-all-trades allowed him to prosper, particularly during the War of 1812 as soldiers frequently passed through the town on the state's main east-west road. Prosperity waned, however, near the end of the war, and by the age of fourteen, Heber was required to work in his father's blacksmith shop. Because of even further financial setbacks, when the youth was nineteen his father told him he was on his own. Said Heber, "I saw some days of sorrow; my heart was troubled, and I suffered much. . . . I found myself cast abroad upon the world without a friend to console my grief. In these heartaching hours I suffered much for want of food and the comforts of life, and many times went two of three days without food to eat."[13]

Hearing of Heber's condition, Charles Kimball, an older brother, took Heber in and taught him the trade of pottery. In time, they moved to Mendon, where another pottery business was started. After finishing his period of training, Heber commenced working for wages, and within six months was able to purchase his brother's business.[14]

One warm summer day while riding through the neighboring town of Victor, young Heber passed a house where a man was working in the yard and of whom he asked a drink of water. The man, heading to the well, called to his house for his daughter, Vilate, to bring out a glass. Heber was struck by the young woman's beauty and grace, and it was not long before Heber found another occasion to pass by

▲ *This field of wild daisies grows in the overflow region of Brigham Young's mill dam.*

◄ *(Opposite page) Remnants of Brigham Young's mill. These rocks were likely from the fireplace in the two-story structure that stood there. The fireplace not only provided warmth, but also doubled as a forge on the first floor for blacksmith-type work.*

HEBER'S VISION

A remarkable event occurred that was witnessed not only by Heber C. Kimball and those in Mendon, but also by Brigham Young as far away as Port Byron. One night after retiring to bed, Heber was awakened by a neighbor, John P. Greene, telling him to come out of his house and see the sight in the heavens. Heber recounts:

It was one of the most beautiful starlight nights, so clear that we could see to pick up a pin. We looked to the eastern horizon, and beheld a white smoke arise toward the heavens; as it ascended it formed itself into a belt, and made a noise like the sound of a mighty wind, and continued southwest, forming a regular bow dipping in the western horizon. After the bow had formed, it began to widen out and grow clear and transparent, of a bluish cast; it grew wide enough to contain twelve men abreast.

In this bow an army moved, commencing from the east and marching to the west; they continued marching until they reached the western horizon. They moved in platoons, and walked so close that the rear ranks trod in the steps of their file leaders, until the whole bow was literally crowded with soldiers. We could distinctly see the muskets, bayonets and knapsacks of the men, who wore caps and feathers like those used by the American soldiers in the last war with Britain; and also saw their officers with their swords and equipage, and the clashing and jingling of their implements of war, and could discover the forms and features of the men. The most profound order existed throughout the entire army; when the foremost man stepped, every man stepped at the same time; I could hear the steps. When the front rank reached the western horizon a battle ensued, as we could distinctly hear the report of arms and the rush.[1]

Heber learned that this heavenly miracle—which may have signified that the army of righteousness would now march forth—appeared on the same night that Joseph received the plates from Moroni on the hill called Cumorah.[2]

1. Orson F. Whitney, *The Life of Heber C. Kimball: An Apostle—The Father and Founder of the British Mission* (Salt Lake City: Bookcraft, 1945), 16.
2. Ibid.

their house . . ."[15] The romance blossomed, and on 7 November 1822, Heber and Vilate were married.

In 1831, Heber and Vilate heard the message of the restored gospel, one and a half years after Samuel Smith left the first Book of Mormon in Mendon. Five elders from The Church of Jesus Christ of Latter-day Saints, having just departed from a small branch in Columbia, came through Mendon and stopped at the home of Phineas Young, where they preached the restored gospel. Through the Holy Spirit, they touched the hearts of their listeners. Both Brigham and Heber were in that audience. Desiring to learn more, in January of 1832 Heber, Brigham, Phineas, and the wives of the latter two, traveled, "amid snow, fording rivers and sometimes crossing on the ice," to meet with the small branch in Columbia, Pennsylvania.[16] Having witnessed manifestations of the gift of tongues, as well as prophecy during the six days they were there, the group returned to Mendon, convinced of the truths taught in the restored gospel.

Soon thereafter, Father Young and sons Phineas and Joseph traveled to Pennsylvania to receive baptism into the new religion. A few months later, on April 15, Eleazer Miller, a convert of only four months, baptized Brigham in the frigid waters of his own mill pond, and, as Brigham records, "before my clothes were dry on my back, he laid his hands on me and ordained me an Elder, at which I marvelled."[17]

The following day, Alpheus Gifford approached Heber while he was forming a vessel on his pottery wheel, and the subject of the gospel arose. Stating his readiness to be baptized, Heber recounted, "I

▶ *(Opposite page) Overlook of Young Property in Mendon. The John Young house continues to stand on the southeast corner of Mendon-Ionia and Cheese Factory Roads.*

▲ In Auburn is the home of William Henry Seward, Abraham Lincoln's Secretary of State. Brigham Young worked as an apprentice during the construction of this mansion. He worked on various parts of the house, including the mantle of the fireplace.

Today, the occupants of virtually every old house in Auburn boast of a Brigham Young mantlepiece, staircase, or semi-elliptical fanlight doorway. A number of these homes also have desks and chairs reputedly made by Brigham.

In the nearby town of Fishers, on Main Street, stands Phineas Young's home, as well as another house built by Brigham.

arose, pulled off my apron, washed my hands and started with him, with my sleeves rolled up to my shoulders, and went a distance of one mile, where he baptized me in a small stream in the woods."[18] Within a few weeks, the wives of both Brigham and Heber would follow them into the waters of baptism.

Being filled with the Holy Ghost, "like a consuming fire,"[19] Brigham and Heber, now fast friends, arranged their affairs so they could preach the word in the regions round about. With Vilate caring for Miriam, the two newly ordained elders planned to visit all of the surrounding towns, "without purse or scrip." They met with some success, but upon returning home, it was apparent that Miriam would not live long, and on 8 September 1832, she died. Brigham placed his two daughters in the care of Heber's wife, Vilate, in order to devote his entire efforts to the spreading of the newfound faith.

A branch of the Church was started in Mendon, which flourished as the gifts of the Spirit, including the gift of tongues, were poured out on the Saints, whose number likely exceeded sixty. Many of the new converts had previously attended the Mendon Baptist church, which lost about one-half of its members to the new faith. With the baptism of Nathan Tomlinson, the inn that had fared so well as a stagecoach stop would now double as a meeting-house for the new branch.[20]

As the branch grew, Heber watched the members, noting their lack of worldly goods:

> Women would come from Victor, a distance of three miles . . . and I have seen them walk barefooted until they came near where I lived, and then they would put on their white stockings and shoes to go into meeting; and when they came out of meeting and

had passed off a little out of sight, they would pull off their shoes and stockings and go home barefooted, for the purpose of saving their fine shoes and stockings they had spun and knit out of flax.[21]

Late in the fall of 1832, Brigham, his brother Joseph, and Heber departed for Kirtland, Ohio, where they first came upon the Prophet Joseph Smith felling trees in the forest. Joseph recognized Brigham as "a man who will yet preside over this Church."[22] The young prophet then, for the first time, heard the gift of tongues as Brigham Young spoke in what was later proclaimed by the Prophet as the Adamic language.[23] When the group returned to Mendon, Brigham reduced his business and belongings even more so that he could spend his time preaching, while Heber, the next year, disposed of his possessions so that he could gather with the Saints in Kirtland.

Prior to leaving, Heber felt the wrath of religious prejudice as unjust claims were made against him, and his goods were seized by officers of the law. With little hope of receiving a fair trial, he settled the false debts. Late in the fall of 1833, the family of Heber C. Kimball, as well as Brigham Young and his two daughters, departed from Mendon by wagon on their way to Ohio.[24] With time, most of the Saints in the Mendon region left behind the lives that they had built and migrated to Kirtland, Ohio, to gather with the Saints.

Today in Mendon, "a bucolic quiet rests over the locality reduced now to a handful of families. Grassy meadows mark sites of former homes."[25] No longer on the major road between Canandaigua and Buffalo, this quiet region will forever be remembered for the unwavering faith of those who lived there.

▲ "There could scarcely be a more kind and affectionate husband and father than [Brigham] was, and few men in his circumstances would have provided better for their families. Mrs. Young was sick, most of the time unable to do any kind of work . . . she was well deserving [of] his care and attention."[26] When Brigham returned from a mission in September of 1832, he found his wife, Miriam, dying. Her last moments were spent praising the Lord.

Endnotes

INTRODUCTION

1. See Amos 3:7 and 8:11; Proverbs 4:19.

2. See Isaiah 9:2.

3. See Matthew 5:17; Ephesians 4:11-12; 1 Corinthians 15: 22-23; and Hebrews 5:9.

4. See also 2 Thessalonians 2:1-2 and 2 Timothy 4:4.

5. See Acts 3:21.

6. Boyd K. Packer, "The Cloven Tongues of Fire," *Ensign* (May 2000), 8.

7. Dr. Tim Dowley, ed., *Eerdman's Handbook to the History of Christianity* (Grand Rapids, Michigan: WM. B. Eerdmans Publishing Co., 1987), 360-363.

8. Joseph Fielding Smith, *Doctrines of Salvation,* comp. Bruce R. McConkie, 3 vols. (Salt Lake City: Bookcraft, 1954-56), 1:174-75. (Infobase)

9. Pearl of Great Price, JSH 1:17.

10. Parley P. Pratt, *Autobiography of Parley P. Pratt,*(Salt Lake City: Deseret Book, 1985), 110-111.

11. Dowley, *Erdman's Handbook,* 352-353; 364-366.

12. John Sorenson, *An Ancient American Setting for the Book of Mormon* (Salt Lake City: Deseret Book, 1996), 30-32.

13. "We interpret [1 Ne.13:12] to refer to Columbus," Gordon B. Hinckley, *Ensign* (November 1992), 52.

14. Joseph Smith, *History of the Church of Jesus Christ of Latter-day Saints,* ed. B. H. Roberts, 7 vols. (Salt Lake City: Deseret Book, 1978), 1:5.

15. Milton V. Backman, *Joseph Smith's First Vision* (Salt Lake City: Bookcraft, 1971), 60-61.

16. As quoted in George E. Condon, *Stars in the Water: The Story of the Erie Canal* (Garden City, New York: Doubleday & Co., Inc., 1974), 165.

17. William W. Phelps, "The Spirit of God," in *Hymns of The Church of Jesus Christ of Latter- Day Saints* (Salt Lake City: The Church of Jesus Christ of Latter-Day Saints, 1985), no. 2.

18. Gordon B. Hinckley, address given in Winnipeg, Manitoba, Canada, 4 August 1998. Quoted in *LDS Church News,* 7 November 1998, 2.

CHAPTER 1

1. John H. Thompson, ed., *Geography of New York State* (Syracuse, New York: Syracuse University Press, 1966), 31.

2. "Finger Lakes Region," *Cayuga County Travel Guide,* Cayuga County Office of Tourism, Auburn, New York, 2.

3. David M. Ellis, James A. Frost, Harold C. Syrett, Harry J. Carman, *A History of New York State* (Ithaca, New York: Cornell University Press, 1967), 3.

4. Ellis, *History of New York State,* 4.

5. Ibid., 16.

6. Backman, *Joseph Smith's First Vision,* 6.

7. Ellis, *History of New York State,* 152-153.

8. Backman, *Joseph Smith's First Vision,* 8.

9. Ellis, *History of New York State,* 154; Backman, *Joseph Smith's First Vision,* 9.

10. Ibid.

11. Backman, *Joseph Smith's First Vision,* 12.

12. Thompson, *Geography of New York,* 143.

13. Ibid., 143-144.

14. Quoted in Thompson, *Geography of New York,* 143.

15. Ibid., 156.

16. Ibid., 143.

17. Blake McKelvey, *A Panoramic History of Rochester and Monroe County, New York* (Woodland Hills, GA: Windsor Publications, 1979), 21-24.

18. George E. Condon, *Stars in the Water: The Story of the Erie Canal* (Garden City, New York: Doubleday & Co., Inc., 1974), 19.

19. Ibid., 126.

Chapter 2

1. Scott and Maurine Proctor, eds., *The Revised and Enhanced History of Joseph Smith by His Mother* (Salt Lake City: Bookcraft, 1996), 81.

2. Richard L. Bushman, *Joseph Smith and the Beginnings of Mormonism* (Urbana and Chicago: University of Illinois Press, 1988), 40.

3. *Church History in the Fulness of Times* (Salt Lake City: Corporation of the President, 1993), 24.

4. Bushman, *Beginnings,* 40, 200.

5. Proctor, *History of Joseph Smith,* 85-86.

6. Backman, *Joseph Smith's First Vision,* 14-15.

7. Larry C. Porter, "A Study of the Origins of The Church of Jesus Christ of Latter-day Saints in the States of New York and Pennsylvania, 1816-1831" (Ph.D. dissertation, Brigham Young University, 1971), 88.

8. Joseph Smith Jr., *Manuscript History of the Church,* Book A-1, Note A, 131-132.

9. Proctor, *History of Joseph Smith,* 86.

10. Ibid.

11. Lucy Smith, *Biographical Sketches of Joseph Smith the Prophet and His Progenitors for Many Generations* (Independence, Missouri: Herald Publishing House, 1969), 87.

12. Ibid., 120-121.

13. Donald Q. Cannon, "Palmyra, New York: 1820-1830," in *Regional Studies in Latter-day Saint Church History/ New York.* Eds. Larry C. Porter, Milton V. Backman Jr. and Susan Easton Black (Provo, Utah: Dept. of Church History and Doctrine, Brigham Young University, 1992), 1-2; Backman, *Joseph Smith's First Vision* (Salt Lake City: Bookcraft, 1971), 34.

14. Ibid., 2.

15. Backman, *Joseph Smith's First Vision,* 39.

16. Proctor, *History of Joseph Smith,* 86.

17. Ibid.

18. Donald L. Enders, "'A Snug Log House': A Historical Look at the Joseph Smith, Sr., Family Home in Palmyra, New York," *Ensign* (August 1985), 17.

19. Enders, "A Snug Log House," 4-8.

20. Porter, "Study of the Origins," 39.

21. Ibid.

22. Porter, "Origins," 41; see also Bushman, *Beginnings,* 47-48.

23. Enders, "The Sacred Grove," *Ensign,* April 1990, 16.

24. Enders, "'A Snug Log House,'" 16.

25. Lucy Smith, *Biographical Sketches,* 70.

26. Enders, "'A Snug Log House,'" 17.

27. Lucy Smith, *Biographical Sketches,* 163.

28. Ibid., 120-121.

29. Dean C. Jessee, ed., *The Personal Writings of Joseph Smith* (Deseret Book: Salt Lake City, 1984), 4-8. (Gospelink)

30. Ellis, *History of New York State,* 164.

31. Jessee, *Writings,* 4-8.

32. Enders, "A Snug Log House," 17.

33. Lucy Smith, *Biographical Sketches,* 71.

34. Enders, "A Snug Log House," 18.

35. Bushman, *Beginnings,* 48.

36. Smith, *History of the Church,* 1:2.

37. Horatio Gates Spafford, *A Gazetteer of the State of New York* (Albany, New York: B.D.Packard, 1824; reprint Interlaken, New York: Heart of the Lake Publishing, 1981), 302.

38. Bushman, *Beginnings,* 44-45.

39. Vicki Bean Topliff, *Willard Bean, The Fighting Parson: The Rebirth of Mormonism in Palmyra* (n.p., 1993), 6-7.

40. Willard Bean Papers (including the autobiography of Willard

Bean). Courtesy of Brigham Young University Archives, 103.

41. Topliff, *Willard Bean, The Fighting Parson,* 57.

42. Ibid., 57.

43. Ibid., 69.

44. Willard Bean Papers, 119.

45. Ibid., 107.

46. Ibid., 113.

CHAPTER 3

1. Enders, "A Snug Log House," 17.

2. Backman, *Joseph Smith's First Vision,* 44.

3. Bushman, *Beginnings,* 55.

4. Smith, *History of the Church,* 1:3.

5. Backman, *First Vision,* 76-77.

6. Ibid, 71-73.

7. "Non-Mormon Editor's Account of the First Vision," Appendix G, in Backman. *First Vision,* 176.

8. "1835 Recital of the First Vision," Appendix B, in Backman, *First Vision,* 158.

9. Smith, *History of the Church,* 1:5.

10. Ibid.

11. Jessee, *Personal Writings,* 4-8.

12. Lucy Smith, *Biographical Sketches,* 84.

13. Jessee, *Personal Writings,* 4-8.

14. Smith, *History of the Church,* 1:2-3.

15. Ibid., 1:4.

16. Ibid.

17. Ibid., 1:5.

18. "1838 Recital," Appendix C, in Backman. *First Vision,* 163; Smith, *History of the Church,* 1:5.

19. "1835 Recital," Appendix B, in Backman, *First Vision,*159.

20. "1838 Recital," Appendix C, in Backman. *First Vision,* 163; Smith, *History of the Church,* 1:5.

21. "1835," in Backman. *First Vision,* 159.

22. Ibid.

23. "Orson Pratt's Account of the First Vision," Appendix E, in Backman, *First Vision,* 172.

24. "1838 Recital," in Backman. *First Vision,* 163; Smith, *History of the Church,* 1:5.

25. "Extract from Wentworth Letter," Appendix D, in Backman, *First Vision,* 169.

26. "1838," in Backman, *First Vision,* 163; Smith, *History of the Church,* 1:5.

27. Pearl of Great Price, JSH, 1:16.

28. "Wentworth," in Backman, *First Vision,* 169.

29. "1832 Recital," Appendix A, in Backman, *First Vision,* 157.

30. "1838," in Backman, in *First Vision,* 163; Smith, *History of the Church,* 1:6.

31. "Wentworth," in Backman, *First Vision,* 169.

32. "1835," in Backman. *First Vision,* 159.

33. "1832," in Backman, *First Vision,* 157.

34. Smith, *History of the Church,* 1:6.

35. Ibid., 1:6.

36. Ibid., 1:7.

37. Ibid., 1:8.

38. Gordon B. Hinckley, Palmyra Temple dedicatory prayer, *Church News,* 15 April 2000, 7.

39. Pearl of Great Price, JSH, 1:16.

CHAPTER 4

1. Smith, *History of the Church,* 1:7.

2. Bushman, *Beginnings,* 59.

3. Proctor, *History of Joseph Smith,* 100.

4. Ibid., 106.

5. Smith, *History of the Church,* 1:9.

6. Oliver Cowdery, ed., *Messenger and Advocate* 1 (October 1834), 70. (Infobase)

7. Smith, *History of the Church,* 1:11-12.

8. Ibid., 1:13.

9. Reeve & Cowan, *Regional Studies,* 79-80.

10. Smith, *History of the Church,* 1:15.

11. Ibid.

12. Oliver Cowdery, ed., *Messenger and Advocate* 1, Oct. 1835, 196. (Infobase)

13. Rex C. Reeve Jr. and Richard O. Cowan, "The Hill Called Cumorah," in *Regional Studies,* 73.

14. Smith, *History of the Church,* 1:13.

15. Reeve and Cowan, *Regional Studies,* 74.

16. Oliver Cowdery, *Messenger and Advocate,* July 1835, 158; October 1835, 197. (Infobase)

17. Smith, *History of the Church,* 1:15-16.

18. Ibid.

19. Ibid.

20. Oliver Cowdery, *Messenger and Advocate,* October 1835, 198. (Infobase)

21. Ibid.

22. Ibid.

23. Lucy Smith, *Biographical Sketches,* 83.

24. Smith, *History of the Church,* 1:16.

25. *Messenger and Advocate,* October 1835, 199. (Infobase)

26. Lucy Smith, *Biographical Sketches,* 85-86.

27. Ibid., 86.

28. Smith, *History of the Church,* 1:15.

29. Lucy Smith, *Biographical Sketches,* 99.

30. Ibid.

31. H. Donl Peterson, "Moroni: Joseph Smith's Teacher," in *Regional Studies,* 63.

32. Smith, *History of the Church,* 4:537.

33. Peterson, *Regional Studies,* 65-67.

34. Richard Lloyd Anderson, "The Alvin Smith Story, Fact and Fiction," *Ensign,* August 1997, 58-72.

35. Proctor, *History of Joseph Smith,* 139.

36. Lucy Smith, *Biographical Sketches,* 104.

36. Ibid., 105.

38. Ibid., 106.

39. Porter, "Origins," 69.

40. Reeve and Cowan, *Regional Studies,* 74-76.

41. *Willard Bean Papers,* 114-117.

42. Reeve and Cowan, *Regional Studies,* 78-80; Porter, "Origins," 71.

43. Reeve and Cowan, *Regional Studies,* 79-80.

44. Ibid., 81-89.

CHAPTER 5

1. Lucy Smith, *Biographical Sketches,* 84.

2. Ibid.

3. Ibid., 88.

4. Smith, *History of the Church,* 5:126-127.

5. *Wayne Sentinel* (Palmyra), 30 September 1824, as quoted in Larry C. Porter, "Organizational Origins of the Church of Jesus Christ, 6 April 1830," in *Regional Studies,* 75-76.

6. Enders, "A Snug Log House," 19.

7. Lucy Smith, *Biographical Sketches,* 92-93.

8. Ibid., 94.

9. Ibid.

10. Ibid., 95-97.

11. Ibid.

12. Pratt, *Autobiography,* 31.

13. Lucy Smith, letter to Mary Pierce, dated 24 January 1829, published in *Ensign* (October 1982), 70-73.

14. Ibid.

15. Joseph Smith, *History of the Church,* 1:11.

16. Proctor, *History of Joseph Smith,* 245.

17. Lucy Smith, *Biographical Sketches,* 167.

18. Dale L. Berge, "Archaeological Work at the Smith Log Cabin," *Ensign* (August 1985), 24- 26.

19. Gordon B. Hinckley, as quoted in Greg Hill's "Pres. Hinckley dedicates historic sites," *Church News,* 4 April, 1998, 6.

20. Boyd K. Packer, *Church News,* 15 April, 2000, 15.

21. Gordon B. Hinckley, Palmyra Temple dedicatory prayer, 7.

22. Gordon B. Hinckley, *Ensign* (May 2000), 107-108.

23. Dave Richards, *Church News,* 15 April, 2000.

CHAPTER 6

1. Emily C. Blackman, *History of Susquehanna County Pennsylvania* (n.p.: Regional Publishing Co., 1970), 25.

2. Ibid., 9.

3. Rhamanthus Stocker, *Centennial History of Susquehanna County, Pennsylvania* (n.p.; Regional Publishing Co. 1974), 1.

4. Blackman, *History*, 103.

5. Ibid., 103-104.

6. Ibid., 103.

7. Joseph Smith, *History of the Church*, 1:17.

8. Lucy Smith, *Biographical Sketches*, 91-92.

9. Joseph Smith, *History of the Church*, 1:17.

10. William G. Hartley, *They Are My Friends: A History of the Joseph Knight Family, 1825- 1850* (Provo, Utah: Grandin Book, 1986), 21.

11. Joseph Smith, *History of the Church*, 1:17.

12. Porter, "Origins," 129.

13. Joseph Smith, *History of the Church*, 1:19.

14. Porter, "Origins," 133.

15. Milton V. Backman, *Eyewitness Accounts of the Restoration* (Orem, Utah: Grandin Book, 1983), 84-85.

16. Ibid.

17. Joseph Smith, *History of the Church*, 1:20.

18. Lucy Smith, *Biographical Sketches*, 118.

19. Ibid., 119-120.

20. Ibid., 120-121.

21. Ibid., 123.

22. Ibid., 124.

23. Proctor, *History of Joseph Smith*, 171.

24. Ibid., 122.

25. See Doctrine and Covenants 10:30.

26. Lucy Smith, *Biographical Sketches*, 125.

27. Bachman, *Eyewitness*, 117.

28. Joseph Smith, *History of the Church*, 1:28.

29. Lucy Smith, *Biographical Sketches*, 124-127.

30. Oliver Cowdery, *Messenger and Advocate* (October 1834), 14. (Infobase)

31. Ibid., 15.

32. Joseph Smith, *History of the Church*, 1:40-41.

33. Ibid., 1:43.

34. Oliver Cowdery, *Messenger and Advocate* (October 1834), 15.

35. Joseph Smith, *History of the Church*, 1:44.

36. See Doctrine and Covenants 27:12.

37. Porter, "Origins," 88.

38. See Doctrine and Covenants 19:26-27.

39. Porter, "Origins," 88.

40. *Church History in the Fulness of Times* (Salt Lake City: Corporation of the President, 1993), 63.

41. Porter, "Origins," 90.

42. Richard Neitzel Holzapfel and T. Jeffery Cottle, *Old Mormon Palmyra and New England* (Santa Ana, California: Fieldbrook Productions, Inc., 1991), 88.

43. Porter, "Origins," 88.

44. Holzapfel and Cottle, *Old Mormon Palmyra*, 88.

45. *Church History in the Fulness of Times*, 64.

46. Bushman, *Beginnings*, 109.

47. Ibid., 110.

48. Dean C. Jessee, "Joseph Knight's Recollection of Early Mormon History," *BYU Studies* 17 (1976-1977), 325-352.

49. *Ensign* (May 2000), 112.

50. Porter, "Origins," 137.

51. Ibid., 92.

CHAPTER 7

1. *History of Seneca County, New York*, comp. Nellie Douglas (Philadelphia: Everts, Ensign & Everts, 1876), 37. In L. Tom Perry Special Collections, Harold B. Lee Library, Brigham Young University, Provo, Utah.

2. Ibid.

3. Horatio Gates Spafford, *A Gazetteer of the State of New York* (Albany, NY: B.D.Packard, 1824; reprinted by Heart of the Lake Publishing, Interlaken, New York, 1981), 171.

4. Porter, "Origins," 224-225.

5. Ibid., 227, 230.

6. Ibid., 234-235.

7. *Church History in the Fullness of Times* (Salt Lake City: Corporation of the President, 1993), 56.

8. Joseph Smith, *History of the Church*, 6:288-289.

9. Ibid., 1:51.

10. Lucy Smith, *Biographical Sketches*, 136-137.

11. Joseph Smith, *History of the Church*, 1:49.

12. Porter, "Origins," 238.

13. See Doctrine and Covenants 14-16.

14. Bushman, *Beginnings*, 104.

15. Ibid., 103.

16. *Church History in the Fullness of Times*, 59.

17. See 2 Nephi 27:12-14 and Ether 5:2-4.

18. Lucy Smith, *Biographical Sketches*, 138.

19. Joseph Smith, *History of the Church*, 1:54.

20. Pratt, *Autobiography*, 31.

21. Lucy Smith, *Biographical Sketches*, 138.

22. Porter, "Origins," 240.

23. Joseph Smith, *History of the Church*, 1:54.

24. Ibid., 1:54.

25. Porter, "Origins," 240.

26. Joseph Smith, *History of the Church*, 1:54.

27. Ibid., 1:54-55.

28. Ibid., 1:55.

29. Lucy Smith, *Biographical Sketches*, 139.

30. Smith, Joseph, *History of the Church*, 1:84-85.

31. Joseph Smith, *History of the Church*, 1:60-61.

22. Ibid., 1:79.

33. Porter, "Origins," 249.

34. Joseph Smith, *History of the Church*, 1:78-79.

35. Ibid.

36. Porter, "Origins," 251.

37. Robert L. Millet, "From Translations to Revelations: Joseph Smith's Translation of the Bible and the Doctrine and Covenants," in *Regional Studies*, 219.

38. Porter, "Origins," 251.

39. See Doctrine & Covenants 45:60.

40. Doctrine and Covenants sections 28, 30, and 32.

41. See Doctrine and Covenants 38:32.

42. Porter, "Origins," 312.

43. Ibid., 316.

44. Porter, "Organizational Origins," 150.

45. Ibid., 151.

CHAPTER 8

1. H.P. Smith, *History of Broome County*, (Syracuse, New York: D. Mason & Co, 1885), 97.

2. Ibid., 96.

3. Ibid., 95.

4. Decker, *A Capsule History of Afton*, 2.

5. James Smith, *History of Chenango and Madison Counties*, 134.

6. Porter, "Origins," 203.

7. Smith, *History of Broome County*, 71-72.

8. William G. Hartley, *They Are My Friends: A History of the Joseph Knight Family, 1825-1850* (Provo, Utah: Grandin Books, 1986), 7-12.

9. Porter, "Origins," 176.

10. Ann Christle Tobey, "The Vermont Sufferers," master's thesis, Columbia University, 1958, 46.

11. Porter, "Origins," 176.

12. James Smith, *History of Chenango and Madison Counties*, 153-154.

13. Porter, "Origins," 184.

14. Hartley, *They Are My Friends*, 12.

15. Ibid., 18-19.

16. Porter, "Origins," 191-192.

17. Hartley, *They Are My Friends*, 18.

18. Porter, "Origins," 184.

19. Ibid., 249.

20. Smith, *History of the Church*, 1:82-83.
21. Ibid., 1:86.
22. Ibid., 1:88-91.
23. Ibid., 1:94.
24. Ibid., 1:95.
25. Porter, "Origins," 203.
26. Joseph Smith, *History of the Church*, 1:109.
27. Porter, "Origins," 222.
28. See D&C 38:32.

CHAPTER 9

1. David Cook, *LDS History and Sites of Mendon, New York* (n.p.: n.p, 1999), 3. Copyright held by Tomlinson Inn.
2. Spafford. *A Gazetteer of the State of New York*, 313.
3. Cook, *Sites of Mendon*, 5.
4. Lucy Smith, *Biographical Sketches*, 153.
5. Ibid.,167.
6. Leonard J. Arrington, *Brigham Young: American Moses* (Urbana and Chicago: University of Illinois Press, 1986), 13.
7. Ibid., 15-16.
8. J Sheldon Fisher. "Brigham Young as a Mendon Craftsman: A Study in Historical Archeology," in *New York History*, published quarterly by the New York State Historical Association. Cooperstown, New York, October, 1980, LXI/4, 435.
9. Cook, *Sites of Mendon*, 4-5.
10. Fisher, "Brigham Young," 436.
11. Arrington, *American Moses*, 17.
12. Ibid.
13. Orson F. Whitney, *The Life of Heber C. Kimball: An Apostle—The Father and Founder of the British Mission* (Salt Lake City: Bookcraft, 1945), 7.
14. Ibid.
15. Ibid., 8.
16. Arrington, *American Moses*, 29.
17. Ibid., 30.
18. Whitney, *The Life of Heber C. Kimball*, 21-22.
19. Ibid., 22.
20. Cook, *Sites of Mendon*, 7.
21. *Journal of Discourses*, 6:132.
22. Whitney, *The Life of Heber C. Kimball*, 28.
23. Ibid., 29.
24. Ibid.
25. Cook, *Sites of Mendon*, 3.
26. Arrington, *American Moses*, 17.

Photo Credits

PAUL E. GILBERT

Front Cover: Overlook from Hill Cumorah
Back Cover: Palmyra Temple
i   Palmyra Temple stained glass
ii   book bindery
vii   Schuler Falls
ix   Cumorah Visitors Center
xi   Niagara Falls
1   Finger Lakes
3   Taughannock Falls
6   Lakeville Barn
8   Richardson Canal House
9   Rochester
12   barn door
15   cobblestone wall detail
16   Smith frame house
18   hewing timbers
22   Four Corners Churches
23   Erie Canal locks
27   light ray Sacred Grove
31   Sacred Grove
32   Sacred Grove in April
33   path in Sacred Grove
34   fence in Sacred Grove
39   Hill Cumorah monument at sunset
40   Hill Cumorah monument autumn
42   cement Book of Mormon
43   aerial drumlin
45   west side of Hill Cumorah
48   birch trees
49   Hill Cumorah monument on hill
51   Palmyra Temple stained glass
52   Alvin Smith grave
53   Smith log cabin interior
55   Smith log cabin
56   Smith log cabin upstairs
57   Smith log cabin back
59   aerial Palmyra Temple, cabin, grove
60   Palmyra Temple spring
61   Kingdom
62   Palmyra Temple stained glass
63   Palmyra Temple dusk
65   Susquehanna River banks
66   Susquehanna River fern detail

67   misty Susquehanna River
68   Hale home foundation site
69   Susquehanna stones
74   Restoration of Aaronic Priesthood
75   Joseph & Emma Smith Harmony home foundation
77   Grandin building
78   press in Grandin building
80   Palmyra bookstore
81   Martin Harris farm
83   open Bible in Peter Whitmer cabin
87   Hathaway Creek
89   Peter Whitmer cabin upper room
90   Peter Whitmer cabin interior
91   Peter Whitmer cabin interior/fireplace
92   Restoration of Melchizedek Priesthood sculpture
94   Kendig Creek
95   Whitmer farmland
98   Pickerell Pond
100   Susquehanna Valley
107   Brigham Young mill site
108   Tomlinson Inn exterior
109   Tomlinson Inn interior
113   Brigham Young property overlook
114   Seward Mansion
114   Seward Mansion entrance

DOUGLAS L. POWELL

Back Cover: Smith log cabin upstairs bed
v   Susquehanna Valley sunset
vii   Seneca Lake
2   Letchworth Upper Falls
4   Genesee Country field
5   Canandaigua skyline
6   rock commemorating treaty
7   Genesee Country sunset w/barn
8   flower detail
11   Smith frame house autumn
13   Wintergreen Hill
14   aerial Harris farm
14   lake-stone house
17   Smith farm in winter
19   Smith well
20   Smith frame house bed
21   Smith frame house kitchen
23   Erie Canal sunset
25   rock wall built by Smith boys
29   Sacred Grove autumn
30   Sacred Grove tree detail
35   Sacred Grove winter
36   Sacred Grove
41   Eight Witnesses detail
45   Joseph & Moroni detail
46   Hill Cumorah monument night
47   Three Witnesses detail
54   Smith log cabin bed
57   Smith log cabin back
58   jail door
63   Palmyra Temple spire
67   misty Susquehanna River
71   Joseph Knight land
72   Lyons central square pavilion
73   Cobblestone schoolhouse
74   Restoration of Aaronic Priesthood monument detail
76   typeset trays in Grandin building
79   infant grave
81   Palmyra bookstore
84   Peter Whitmer cabin
86   Seneca Lake
87   Fayette Chapel

88   Peter Whitmer cabin bed
93   Hathaway Creek dam
97   Susquehanna Valley
99   Susquehanna River Colesville
102   Josiah Stowell home
103   Tarbell mantle
104   Josiah Stowell grave
105   wilderness between Colesville & Harmony
110   Brigham Young mill remnants
111   wild daisies at Brigham Young mill
115   Miriam Works Young grave

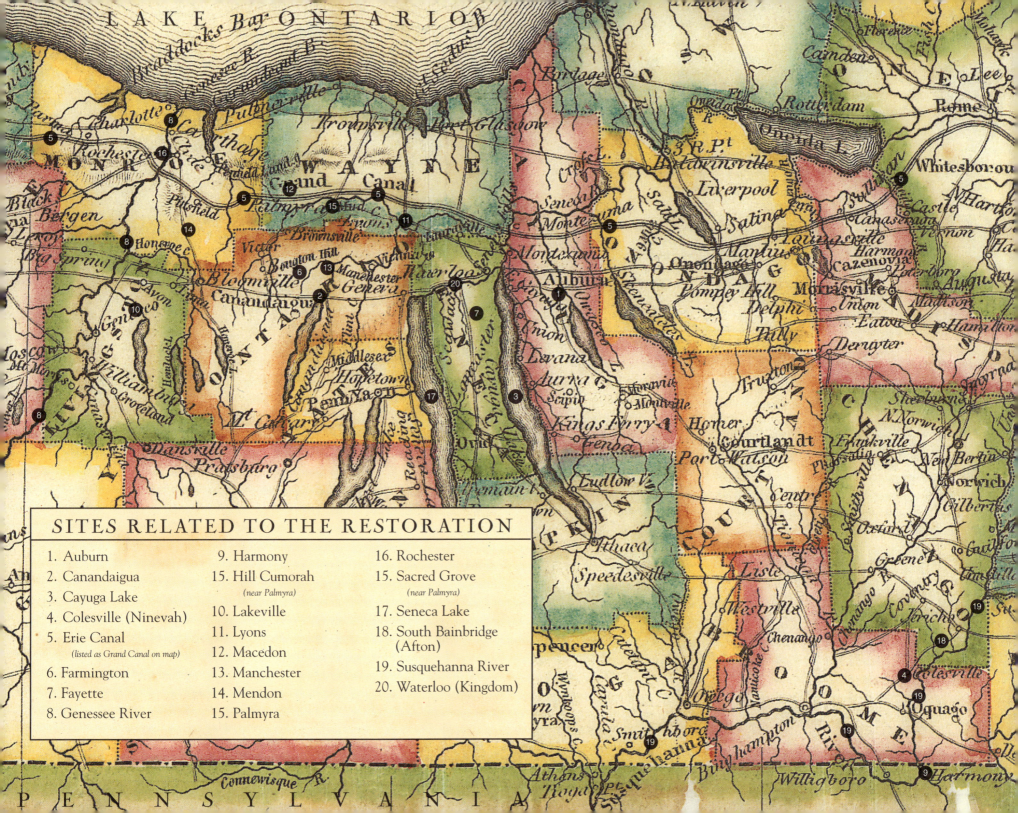

SITES RELATED TO THE RESTORATION

1. Auburn
2. Canandaigua
3. Cayuga Lake
4. Colesville (Ninevah)
5. Erie Canal
   (listed as Grand Canal on map)
6. Farmington
7. Fayette
8. Genessee River

9. Harmony
15. Hill Cumorah
    (near Palmyra)
10. Lakeville
11. Lyons
12. Macedon
13. Manchester
14. Mendon
15. Palmyra

16. Rochester
15. Sacred Grove
    (near Palmyra)
17. Seneca Lake
18. South Bainbridge
    (Afton)
19. Susquehanna River
20. Waterloo (Kingdom)